THE SHORTEST HISTORY OF SCOTLAND

AF583625

Also in this series

The Shortest History of Europe by John Hirst
The Shortest History of England by James Hawes
The Shortest History of China by Linda Jaivin
The Shortest History of Democracy by John Keane
The Shortest History of the Soviet Union by Sheila Fitzpatrick
The Shortest History of Greece by James Heneage
The Shortest History of War by Gwynne Dyer
The Shortest History of India by John Zubrzycki
The Shortest History of the World by David Baker
The Shortest History of the Crown by Stephen Bates
The Shortest History of Economics by Andrew Leigh
The Shortest History of Italy by Ross King
The Shortest History of Japan by Lesley Downer
The Shortest History of Music by Andrew Ford
The Shortest History of Ancient Rome by Ross King
The Shortest History of AI by Toby Walsh
The Shortest History of Scandinavia by Mart Kuldkepp
The Shortest History of Turkey by Benjamin C. Fortna
The Shortest History of Australia by Mark McKenna
The Shortest History of the United States of America by Don Watson
The Shortest History of Innovation by Andrew Leigh
The Shortest History of Ireland by James Hawes

THE SHORTEST HISTORY OF SCOTLAND

MURRAY PITTOCK

Published by Black Inc.,
an imprint of Schwartz Books Pty Ltd
Wurundjeri Country
22–24 Northumberland Street
Collingwood VIC 3066, Australia
enquiries@blackincbooks.com
www.blackincbooks.com

First published in Great Britain in 2026 by Old Street Publishing Ltd
Notaries House, Exeter EX1 1AJ
www.oldstreetpublishing.co.uk

Copyright © Murray Pittock 2026
Murray Pittock asserts his right to be known as the author of this work.

ALL RIGHTS RESERVED
No part of this publication may be reproduced, stored in a retrieval system, or transmitted in any form by any means electronic, mechanical, photocopying, recording or otherwise without the prior consent of the publishers.

9781760645359 (paperback)
9781743824412 (ebook)

A catalogue record for this book is available from the National Library of Australia

Cover design by Beau Lowenstern
Typesetting by Thomas Bohm, User Design, Illustration and Typesetting
Illustrations and maps © James Nunn 2025
Cover image: Bourbon-88 / VectorStock

Every effort has been made to contact the copyright holders of material in this book. However, where an omission has occurred, the publisher will gladly include acknowledgement in any future edition.

Printed in Australia by McPherson's Printing Group.

For Martin Procházka, Mirka Horová,
Petra Johana Poncarová and all the
friends of Scotland in Prague

~

Self-confidence is not pride. Just the contrary: only a person or a nation that is self-confident, in the best sense of the word, is capable of listening to others, accepting them as equals, forgiving its enemies and regretting its own guilt.

Václav Havel, New Year's Address to the Nation,
1 January 1990

And having seen it I accuse
The crested animal in his pride,
Arrayed in all the royal hues
Which hide the claws he well can use
To tear the heart out of the side.

Edwin Muir, 'The Combat'

CONTENTS

EARLY SCOTTISH KINGS

MONARCHS WITH OVERLORDSHIP OVER MOST OF PRESENT-DAY SCOTLAND

Bridei III (r. 672–93)

Óengus I (r. 729/32–61)

Causantín [Constantine] MacFergusa (r. 789–820)

Óengus II (r. 820–32)

Cináed [Kenneth] MacAilpin (r. 841–58)

Domnall I (r. 858–62)

Causantín I mac Cináeda (r. 863–77)

Áed mac Cináeda (r. 877–78)

Giric mac Dúngail (r. 878–89), possibly with Eochaid

Domnal II mac Causantín (r. 889–900)

SCOTTISH MONARCHS

Causantín II [Constantine] Mac Áeda (r. 900–43)

Máel Coluim [Malcolm] mac Domnall (r. 943–54)

Ildulb [Indulf] mac Causantín (r. 954–62)

Dubh (r. 962–67)

Cuilén mac Indulb (r. 967–71)

Amlaíb mac Indulb (r. 971–77)

Cináed II mac Mail Choluim (r. 971/77–95)

Causantín III mac Cuiléin (r. 995–97)

Cináed III mac Duib (r. 997–1005)

Máel Coluim II (r. 1005–34)

Donnchád I [Duncan] mac Crínain (r. 1034–40)

Mac Bethad [Macbeth] mac Findláich (r. 1040–57)

Lulach (r. 1057–58)

Máel Coluim III mac Donnchada (r. 1058–93)

Domhnall III mac Donnchada (r. 1093–94; 1094–97)

Donnchád II mac Máel Choluim (r. 1094)

Edgar (r. 1097–1107)

Alexander I (r. 1107–24)

David I (r. 1124–1153)

Malcolm IV (r. 1153–1165)

William I (r. 1165–1214)

Alexander II (r. 1214–1249)

Alexander III (r. 1249–1286)

Margaret, Maid of Norway (r. 1286–1290)

Interregnum (1290–1292)

John Balliol (r. 1292–1296)

Interregnum (1296–1306)

SCOTTISH MONARCHS (CONT.)

Robert I (r.Bruce) (r. 1306–1329)

David II (r. 1329–1371)

Robert II (r. 1371–1390)

Robert III (r. 1390–1406)

James I (r. 1406–1437)

James II (r. 1437–1460)

James III (r. 1460–1488)

James IV (r. 1488–1513)

James V (r. 1513–1542)

Mary I (r. 1542–1567)

James VI (r. 1567–1603)

JACOBITE CLAIMANTS

James II and VII (r. 1690–1701)

James III and VIII (r. 1701–66)

Charles III (r. 1766–88)

Henry IX (r. 1788–1807)

ENGLISH MONARCHS

Edward I (r. 1272–1307)

Edward II (r. 1307–1327)

Edward III (r. 1327–1377)

Richard II (r. 1377–1399)

Henry IV (r. 1399–1413)

Henry V (r. 1413–1422)

Henry VI (r. 1422–1461, 1470–1471)

Edward IV (r. 1461–1470, 1471–1483)

Edward V (r. 1483)

Richard III (r. 1483–1485)

Henry VII (r. 1485–1509)

Henry VIII (r. 1509–1547)

Edward VI (r. 1547–1553)

Mary I (r. 1553–1558)

Elizabeth I (r. 1558–1603)

HOUSE OF STUART

James I (r. 1603–1625)

Charles I (r. 1625–49)

Interregnum (1651–53)

Commonwealth (1653–60)

Charles II (r. 1649/60–85). Crowned King of Scots 1651

James II & VII (r. 1685–88/90)

Mary & William II & III (r. 1689–94, 1689–1702)

Anne (r. 1702–14)

HOUSE OF HANOVER, SAXE-COBURG-GOTHA AND WINDSOR

George I (r. 1714–1727)
George II (r. 1727–1760)
George III (r. 1760–1820)
George IV (r. 1820–1830)
William IV (r. 1830–1837)
Victoria (r. 1837–1901)
Edward VII (r. 1901–1910)
George V (r. 1910–1936)
Edward VIII (r. 1936)
George VI (r. 1936–1952)
Elizabeth II (r. 1952–2022)
Charles III (r. 2022–)

PREFACE

There are plenty of histories of Scotland on the market. I have even written one or two of them myself. What possible reason could there be to add another?

There is one overriding motive. History is the best guide to the future we have, and people – including people in positions of power – are increasingly ignorant of it. In an age of tribalism, extremes and emotional posturing, knowledge of the past is more important than ever, because it remains absolutely true that forgetting our history is the shortest route to repeating it. The *Shortest History* series produces books that are inexpensive, accessible, clear and to the purpose. In an afternoon they can provide the information to change the beliefs of a lifetime. We need history, we need good history and we need history that is accessible and affordable.

It is a big claim to say that the past foretells the future. In 1992, I was sitting in a bar near Inverness when a medieval historian informed me that the conflict arising from the collapse of Yugoslavia would only end when NATO was bombing Belgrade. At the time, the likelihood of this event seemed remote, yet it duly took place seven years later. In early 2022, when many Europeans were dismissing the possibility of an invasion of Ukraine by Russia, anyone who had read imperial Austrian reports on the Russification carried out in Lemberg (Lviv) in 1916, or Robert Conquest's harrowing *Harvest of Sorrow* (1986), on the Russian genocide in Ukraine in the 1930s, would have had fewer doubts. A year later, not many were willing to see the brutal attack by Hamas, and Israel's brutal response to it, in the context of the previous 75 years. Yet that struggle has long been marked by the unbounded hostility of extremists towards moderate supporters of a two-state solution – and history shows us that believing you have God on your side often licenses the worst of human behaviour in war.

In short: the world is a dangerous place, and ignorance will not make it safer. We all need history.

CHAPTER 1

SCOTLAND BEFORE SCOTLAND

Scotland is unusual. It is one of the oldest nations in Europe, with the most stable borders. Its territory is fundamentally unchanged since the fifteenth century, and its southern border with England has barely altered – apart from Berwick and a few square kilometres of 'debatable' land – since 1237. Scotland's survival as a national entity is worthy of comment: most former historical states have no remaining institutions, jurisdictions or national identity. Scotland does.

And yet Scotland is not a nation state at all. Even the state of which it is a component – the 'United Kingdoms', established by the Union of 1707 – has seen major changes to its borders in relatively recent times, notably through the establishment of the Irish Free State (1922) and later Republic of Ireland (1949). Yet Scotland, despite its apparent marginality, has often been central to British, European and indeed global history, even as the world at large – and much of its own population – has remained ignorant of its achievements.

Land of Mountain and Flood

Ten thousand years ago, Scotland didn't exist. No one thought of it as a separate place and the same was no doubt true of Britain, which only became separate from the rest of Europe after the submergence of Doggerland, the area that joined the Thames to the Rhine, in the seventh millennium BC. The island of Dogger Bank – almost the size of Wales – survived some 100 kilometres off the eastern coast for another two millennia until it, too, was submerged. For a long time afterwards, Britain was neither the island we know nor a place we would easily recognise. 'Neolithic Britain' is as inaccurate a label as 'Neolithic Scotland', if any common ethnicity or culture is intended by those terms. There were many different societies on the main island, and they did not conform to its later internal borders.

The fact that Scotland became a nation at all, with the distinct achievements, culture and memory that have long marked it out, is the outcome of geography and landscape, as well as the history of other places. For centuries, the line of the Forth and Clyde rivers was seen as dividing the island in two, so narrow was the land and so impassable. And Scotland was never Romanised, with the walls marking the northern frontier of the Roman Empire. More than a thousand years later, Matthew Paris's mid-thirteenth-century map shows Scotland as two separate islands joined by a single bridge at Stirling. Apart from the narrow neck of land there, surrounded by marsh and swamp, only the east coast was open to an invading force beyond Forth–Clyde. This was as true for the armies of Henry VIII as for those of Agricola. Beyond the rivers, the towns and their environs, Scotland was largely impenetrable until the eighteenth century.

Difficult to infiltrate by land because of its waterways, bogland and mountains, Scotland was also challenging to secure from the sea. It is a country with a vast, 10,000-km coastline (more than twice the length of England's) with almost as many more thousands of kilometres again in seacoast from its near-800 islands. For most of Scotland's history, transport was most effective by water. Sea travel predominated in the west in particular, where the links with the Isle of Man and Ireland continued into the eighteenth century.

Scotland's impenetrability, its northerly climate and rugged landscape of mountains, forests, rivers and sea helped to steer the

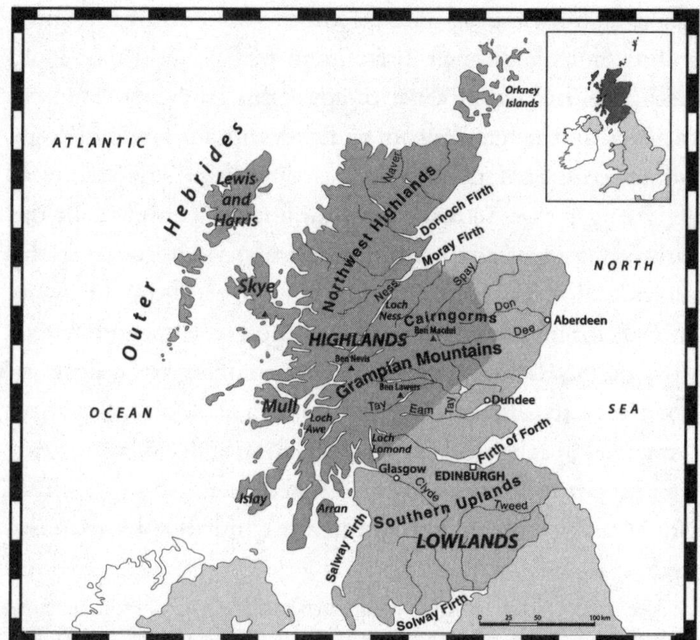

development of a separate nation with a distinct set of cultures in the north of Britain. The Enlightenment notion that Scotland's history and geography are inextricably linked is summed up neatly by Sir Walter Scott in *The Lay of the Last Minstrel*:

> O Caledonia! stern and wild,
> Meet nurse for a poetic child!
> Land of the heath and shaggy wood,
> Land of the mountain and the flood,
> Land of my sires! what mortal hand
> Can e'er untie the filial band
> That knits me to thy rugged strand!

The place that became Scotland was entirely covered with glaciers in the last Ice Age. When the ice receded, the landscape it left was often bare and bleak, home to numerous wild animals, not least wolves, bear, aurochs and lynx – both the country and its fauna had much in common with Scandinavia. Pine, birch, oak and hazel began to cover this landscape. Hunter-gatherer and fisher peoples were present in Scotland from before 10,000 BC, perhaps first settling in the islanded west and living in caves or tents, nomadic but well equipped. By the early fifth millennium BC, simple farming had begun, with the growing of plants (without crop rotation) and the rearing of animals for meat. A wide variety of tools were manufactured, with axe heads found in significant numbers as far apart as Loch Tay and Orkney. Basic pottery also made an appearance. Dreghorn in Ayrshire, with a population today of 3,500, may well have been continuously occupied since 3500 BC, which would make it the oldest continuously inhabited settlement in these islands.

We know little about what the people who lived in pre-Roman Scotland thought and believed about who they were. We do know a good deal about them from their material remains, however, in terms of both the style of their artefacts and the complexity of their housing. It is clear that burial practices varied across the country, as did the buildings associated with religious ceremonies, which tended in the south to be henges and in the north to be stone circles. The Calanais (or Callanish) complex in Lewis and the Ring of Brodgar in Orkney are perhaps the most famous, but there are also many of these monuments in the north-east.

In both Aberdeenshire and Perthshire, large buildings have been found from around 3600 BC: the northern longhouse at Balbridie covers an area of about 240 square metres, almost the size of a tennis court. Domestic architecture on a more intimate scale also survives. Skara Brae on Orkney is a small Neolithic township consisting of ten stone houses, each no larger than

Calanais/Callanish standing stones

a modern one-bedroom flat, protected and framed by earthen walls, with stone furniture and a basic drainage system to let human waste flow into the sea. The furniture is also made of stone and includes recessed beds – these remained a feature of Scottish domestic architecture into the nineteenth century.

The most complete such settlement in Europe, Skara Brae was first occupied before 3000 BC, a few centuries later than the nearby Knap of Howar, the oldest standing building in northern Europe. Their inhabitants were mostly pastoralist farmers who cultivated barley among other grains, kept sheep and cattle, and ate many varieties of shellfish. Deep-sea fishing was also not unknown at Skara Brae, judging by the remains found there. The pottery ('grooved ware') used in the islands was common to groups across northern Scotland. Other material relics of the earliest people in the area include the vast chambered cairn at Maes Howe (2800 BC), built from stone blocks weighing many tonnes, which indicates that a complex ritual life had already developed in Orkney.

Bronze was smelted in Scotland from about 2000 BC.

Cairn at Maes Howe as it appeared soon after being opened in 1861

There was extensive metal working along the river valleys in what is now Aberdeenshire in particular. Trade was needed to acquire the tin for bronze, the closest sources lying in Scandinavia and more distant Cornwall. Wheeled transport is evident from at least 1000 BC, while trade across the North Sea to what is now Germany was underway by the dawn of the Iron Age a few centuries later. The people of northern Britain built wattle and daub houses (later called 'sticks an rice' in the north-east) up to seven metres in diameter. Protected

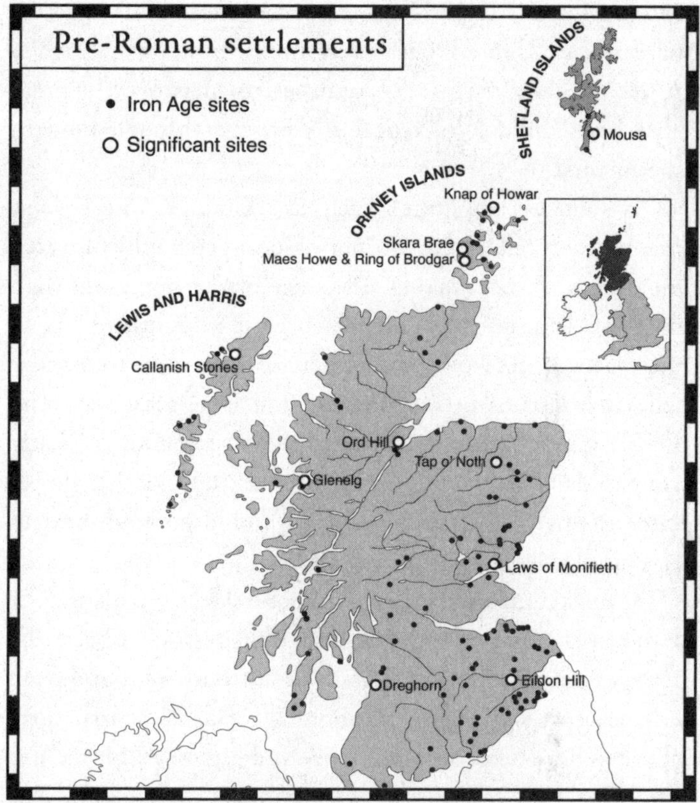

groups of these buildings evolved into hillfort complexes. The largest could be very substantial, such as the hillfort at Eildon Hill, where some 500 houses were spread over an area more than twenty times the size of Celtic Park football ground. The majority of Scotland's more than 1,500 hillforts are just a fraction of this size.

The wood-and-stone walls of these forts – into which livestock could be herded in the face of a threat – might be up to five metres thick, protecting a population of as many as 4,000 (Tap o' Noth in Aberdeenshire) or more, plus their animals. Many of these hillforts, including Ord Hill near Inverness and

Laws of Monifieth near Dundee, survive. Dozens are vitrified, their stone walls fused together by intense heat, possibly when the site was razed by invaders or otherwise destroyed by fire – it has been difficult to repeat the process through modern experiments.

Like smaller structures such as crannogs and brochs, these hillforts reflect the distinctive local geography of water, mountain and rock, taking advantage of the numerous high points of defensible ground which exist in Scotland. As in other parts of the world, the first human attempts to manage their environment in a systematic and large-scale way tend to echo the particular qualities of those surroundings. Later strongholds – for example the fifth-century Pictish power centre at Rhynie in Aberdeenshire – would grow up next to these more ancient rocky fortifications.

The terrain inspired other architectural features distinctive to the area. One was the hollow-walled stone tower, the broch, mainly but not solely built in northern Scotland from perhaps as early as 400 BC to about AD 200. These structures appear to have been both defensive and highly visible centres of prestige: they can be seen as ancestors of the medieval and early-modern tower house. Several hundred were built, five of which – in Lewis, Glenelg, Shetland and Sutherland – retain most of their surviving walls, which rise to more than six metres in some cases (Mousa in Shetland is more than twice this height). Given the thickness of the walls – anywhere from three to five metres deep – the internal area of even the largest broch would have had a footprint no bigger than a modest modern apartment. Inhabitants probably lived mostly on the first floor, where the hearth was.

Crannogs, constructed throughout Scotland and Ireland in this era, were another highly defensible type of building. These dwellings might be mounds of stone (particularly in the Outer Hebrides) or timber. They were built on a wooden platform some 10–30 metres across, or even entire artificial islands. The peak period for crannogs in Scotland largely coincides with that of the broch, though the crannogs may have been inhabited to a much later date. There are some 1,200 recognised sites in Ireland and a third as many in Scotland, suggesting early cultural overlap. (In Wales, by contrast, only one much later example survives.) Their relics may appear humble, but they were probably high-status buildings, providing a secure base for powerful landowners and sub-kings.

The Romans

The greatest empire of the ancient world played a major role in creating the Scotland we know today, if only because the territory lay just outside imperial boundaries for all but the briefest of periods. The northern part of the island was more involved with Roman power and culture than was once thought, but it was never incorporated into the imperial provincial system. Nor did its tribal rulers fall reliably into the looser – but still implicitly subject – category of *rex sociusque et amicus* (allied king and friend).

Julius Caesar raided the south of the island in 55 and 54 BC, but the first full-scale formal Roman invasion of southern Britain took place in AD 43, when Senator Aulus Plautius led more than 20,000 men, with as many more auxiliary troops, to invade from the south coast. Eleven tribal kings surrendered at Camulodunum (Colchester) before the year was out. Rome did not stop there. Three decades later, Governor Vettius Bolanus (in office AD 69–71) may have entered what is now Scotland, which would suggest the Roman timbers found at Carlisle date from AD 72, the year after a fort was established at York. Soon there were a hundred fortified Roman positions in the north of England.

Gnaeus Julius Agricola (AD 40–93) became governor of the province of Britannia in AD 78, and he is traditionally credited with the successful invasion of Scotland. This began in the area south of the Forth in AD 80. Agricola also sent his fleet round Scotland's northern coast, demonstrating that Britain as a whole was an island. In AD 83, he crossed the Forth–Clyde line with some 25,000 men in a serious attempt to invade Scotland up the east coast and extend the 16-km fortified line known as the Gask Ridge into the far north and the Caledonian highlands. He eventually reached as far as the Moray coast by Inverness, where his main enemy were the *Caledonii*, spearheading tribal resistance to Rome.

Agricola's force defeated the host of Caledonians and their allies at Mons Graupius. The site has still not been definitively identified but may well be Bennachie in northern Aberdeenshire, from where the tribal forces would have had the advantage of attacking from high ground. Though the Romans won the battle, they had required a substantial army to do so. Winning the war was a different matter. The historian Tacitus, who also happened to be Agricola's son-in-law, accused the Emperor Domitian of recalling the governor out of jealousy so the conquest of Scotland could not be completed, but demand for troops in Dacia (Romania) is perhaps the more likely reason. Either way, the considerable expenditure on maintaining troops in the north was surely out of all proportion to any assets acquired through conquest.

Tacitus' quip that '*perdomita Britannia et statim missa*' ('Britannia was no sooner conquered than let go') was an exaggeration, as are many other aspects of his account. Nevertheless, he gave us the name of the first (alleged) historical Scottish patriot, Calgacus, ostensibly a Caledonian chieftain at Mons Graupius. While Calgacus may be entirely fictional, the name does have a potential Gaelic cognate in *calgach* – meaning prickly, piercing, passionate: all terms for a swordsman. Tacitus grants his hero some stirring republican rhetoric in keeping with the historian's own suspicion of the empire, including what is perhaps his most famous line, '*ubi solitudinem faciunt pacem appellant*' – '(every)where they make a desert and call it peace' – a pithy critique of imperialism that has resounded down the centuries.

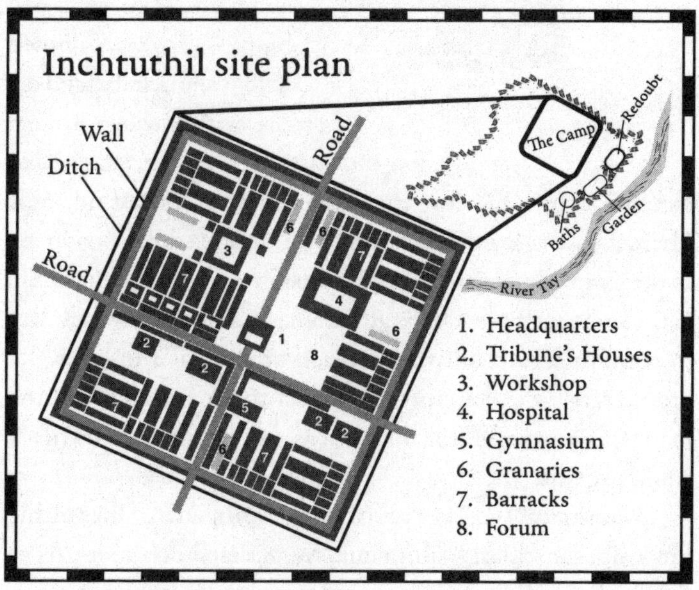

The temporary nature of Agricola's success was soon visible at scale. Substantial Roman forts were erected to block advances from the northern glens. Inchtuthil, south-west of Blairgowrie, covered nearly 22 hectares and contained some sixty-six barrack blocks. Defended by a six-metre-wide, two-metre-deep ditch, behind which stood a rampart six metres

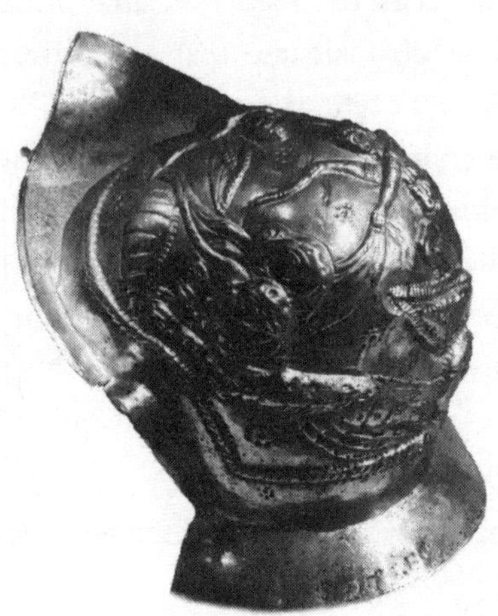

Bronze helmet excavated at the Roman fort of Trimontium, near Newstead

tall, this fort alone could accommodate a legion of more than 5,000 infantry, plus a few auxiliaries. Tellingly, it also had hospital accommodation for 300 men. Despite its vast size and the cost of building and garrisoning it, Inchtuthil was abandoned almost as soon as it was built – 750,000 unused nails were left behind by the withdrawing Roman forces. A generation later, material at the big fort at Trimontium (at Newstead, near Melrose in the Borders) was likewise destroyed or abandoned as the Emperor Trajan recalled Roman troops to the European mainland to fight in Dacia. A pattern had been set which was to continue: Scotland was in reach of Roman arms, but at a prohibitive cost. It simply tied down too many men and too many resources for the limited assets its difficult territory could provide.

Over thirty years later and over 250 km south of Inchtuthil, the wall that still bears his name was erected on the orders of the Roman Emperor Hadrian (r. 117–38). Begun in AD 122, Hadrian's Wall stretches 120 km from coast to coast. In places it reached up to four metres in height, with a deep ditch immediately to the south of the wall. Its seventeen large forts (there were also eighty smaller mile-castles, the Roman mile being 10 per cent shorter than the English one) could hold almost two legions: about 10,000 men, or around 6 per cent of Rome's entire standing army. Built to secure the permanent northern frontier, it was the largest border defence force in the Roman Empire.

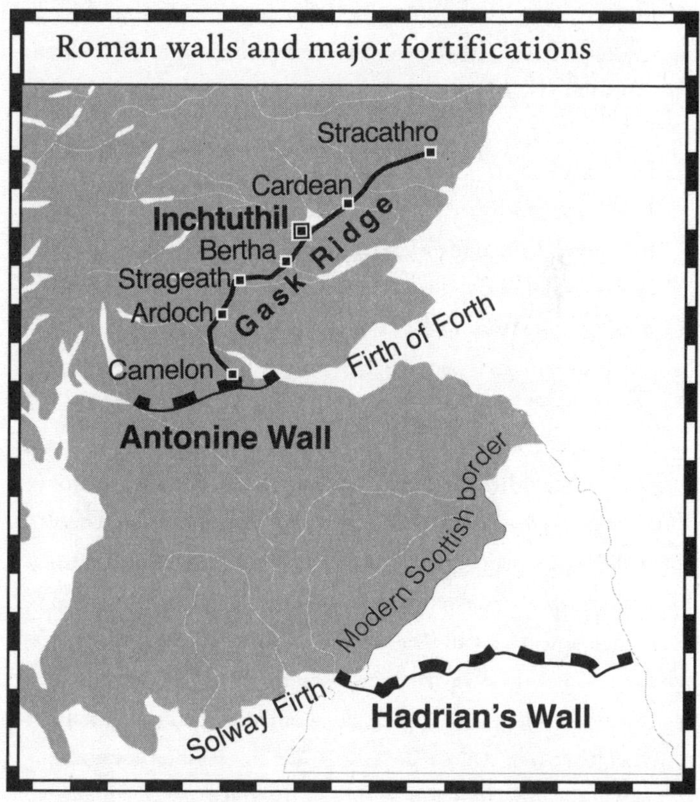

Roman walls and major fortifications

In 142, Hadrian's successor Antonius Pius (r. 138–61) authorised an invasion by the second, sixth and twentieth legions to move up to the Forth–Clyde line and build a second wall there between Cramond and Old Kilpatrick. This was a major undertaking: only four legions were assigned to guard the entire Rhine frontier. The Antonine Wall was finished twelve years later. Almost exactly half the length of Hadrian's Wall and made of turf, it was constructed to a cheaper specification, though still with enough accommodation for 13,000 infantry or 6,500 cavalry. As with Inchtuthil, however, it was barely finished before it fell into disuse. Even before Emperor Antonius died in 161, there were thoughts of abandoning it, and in the decade after his death Roman troops pulled out. Withdrawal was complete by 169.

Hadrian's Wall

Vallum Aelium (the 'Wall of Aelius', after part of Hadrian's full name) divided the island in two, between an area that was Romanised and one that – for the most part – was not. The Wall was one reason why different countries developed to its north and south: indeed, there was a tradition in the medieval period that the boundary was erected much later, following an invasion of the Picts and Scots in the fourth century.

There are other reasons, to be sure, for the development of a Scottish nation in earlier ages, such as Scotland's closeness to Ireland and the superiority of sea to land communications, but the Wall remains central in our consciousness and language to this day. The whole of Hadrian's great frontier fortress lies deep in what is now England – but when we say 'north of the Wall', it is always Scotland that is meant. The Roman province 'Britannia' never included anything of what is now Scotland, except in fits and starts. Even after the departure of the Romans, to be *Bretwalda* – sovereign of Britain – meant to be overlord of the Roman province east of Offa's Dyke and south of the Wall, not the whole island. The confusion that existed – and to an extent, continues to exist – between the Roman province of Britannia and the island of Britain long made the Kingdom of Scotland an ambiguous entity in English eyes, both a separate country and one over which they intermittently claimed lordship.

Thus the Wall effectively divided the island into two parts: Roman Britannia to the south; and the land of the Caledonians, Picts and later Scots to the north. The core of that territory, north of the Antonine line of Forth–Clyde, would later be termed the Kingdom of Alba, and would form the heartland of modern Scotland.

Some historians interpret the imposing majesty of the Hadrianic frontier in particular as a statement of imperial power, but the truth of the matter is surely plain to see. At the Gask Ridge and the Antonine Wall, Rome had created frontiers that devoured money and manpower urgently needed elsewhere. With the natives unquestionably restless, it was not long before the cost of holding onto them began to seem too high.

A last effort at conquest was made by Septimius Severus (r. 193–211), who came in person in AD 208. Severus' base at a rebuilt Trimontium extended to 66 hectares, an indication of the size of his force. Some historians believe this was as large as 40,000 men (including auxiliaries), which would put it roughly on a par with the army mounted to invade Britannia in AD 43. Severus moved his force to Carpow to the south of the Tay, then probed north. The Caledonians yielded territory in return for money, presumably confident that they would gain the latter immediately and could regain the former at leisure. In this they proved to be correct: when Severus died at York, the town of Corbridge, over 120 km south of the Tweed, remained the most northerly Roman settlement on the east coast. Severus' son and successor Caracalla (r. 198–217) once again abandoned the land north of Hadrian's Wall.

When Severus attacked what is now Scotland, his chief enemies in the north were the *Calidones* and the *Maiatae*, whose names survive in placenames such as Dunkeld, 'fortress

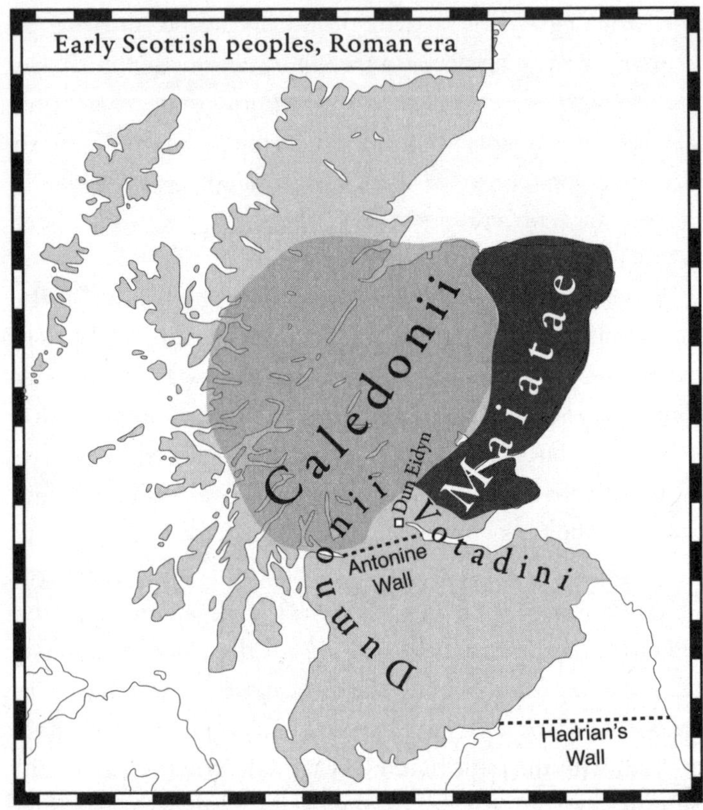

of the Caledonians', and Myothill. The Maiatae appear to have been related to the *Dumnoni* group of peoples whose territories stretched from Westmorland to central Scotland. Placenames that include the name of a people can indicate frontier status, and it is possible that Dunkeld in mid-Perthshire was close to the southern border of the Caledonians.

The *Votadini* were another tribal group identified by Rome on the east coast of Scotland. They later reappear as the Gododdin, whose unsuccessful raid on what was perhaps a largely Saxon camp at Catraeth (Catterick) around 600 is the subject of the early poem '*Y Gododdin*', set in Scotland and northern England but written in a language much closer to modern Welsh: '*Hwn yw e gododdin, aneirin ae cant*' ('This is the Gododdin, Aneirin sang it'). The 'gleaming blue blades' and 'gold-bordered garments' of the men in the poem who 'went to Catraeth / Mead-nourished war-host, strong, vigorous ... close-ranked, stubborn' conjure up striking images of the warriors of Scotland-before-Scotland in combat.

By 600, the Votadini had established their capital at Dun Eidyn (Edinburgh), but their Roman-era stronghold was the great 18-hectare hillfort complex at Traprain Law (or Dunpelder, as it was traditionally known) close to modern Haddington in East Lothian. From here they traded with the Roman world to the south: a large hoard of fourth-century Roman silver has been found in the fortress.

Traprain Law treasure: part of a silver plate showing Venus rising from the waves, AD 410–425

By the end of the third century, the Romans were calling the inhabitants of the country north of the Forth or Tay rivers *Picti* (the painted ones). Increasingly they thought of these Picts as an entirely separate people from other Britons, though this may have owed more to the presence of their own wall than to any pre-existing state of affairs. The Romans also now became aware of another people in the west of Scotland, who spoke a different language. By the fourth century these were identified as the *Scoti* – the Roman historian Ammianus Marcellinus (*c.* 330–*c.* 400), for example, wrote of 'Scots and Picts' – and their language was an early form of Gaelic. The word that was to give the country its eventual name thus made its first appearance just as Hadrian's Wall began to be abandoned by the Romans, a process that was complete by AD 400.

Enter the Scots

The Scoti lived along the western coasts and on the islands of Scotland, but they shared a heritage with the inhabitants of Ireland. Indeed, until the twelfth century, the Irish were often called 'Scoti' by Continental Europeans, and many Irish myths and stories, such as those of Cú Chulainn and Fionn, were partly set in what is now Scotland. It has long been posited that armed invasion from Ireland was the origin of the western kingdoms of these Scots, but one should be wary of crude narratives of ethno-cultural displacement and the modern assumptions that underlie them. Many Scottish families – Clan Donald (Clann Dòmhnaill) is perhaps the clearest example – had historical links across the few sea miles separating Ireland from Kintyre. The water was probably not a simple frontier crossed by an invading force, but a porous threshold between two lands. In the eastern of these, the Scottish kingdoms gradually formed.

By 576, Áedán MacGabráin was king in both South Argyll in Scotland and in North Antrim across the water. His

Gabráin kinfolk (Cénel Gabráin) were becoming established over a large territory, as were Cénel Loairn (the Lorne kinfolk). At times these two broad groupings were more or less independent kingdoms, while at others they were both subject to Pictish overlordship. By 700, Cénel Loairn effectively ruled Dál Riata, the lands of the Gaelic-speaking Scots in the west, which included the 130-km stretch of Argyll from Kintyre to Oban, as well as many of the islands on the western seaboard as far north as Mull. There remained a significant connection between Picts and Scots, as the persistence of hybrid Pictish and Gaelic names shows.

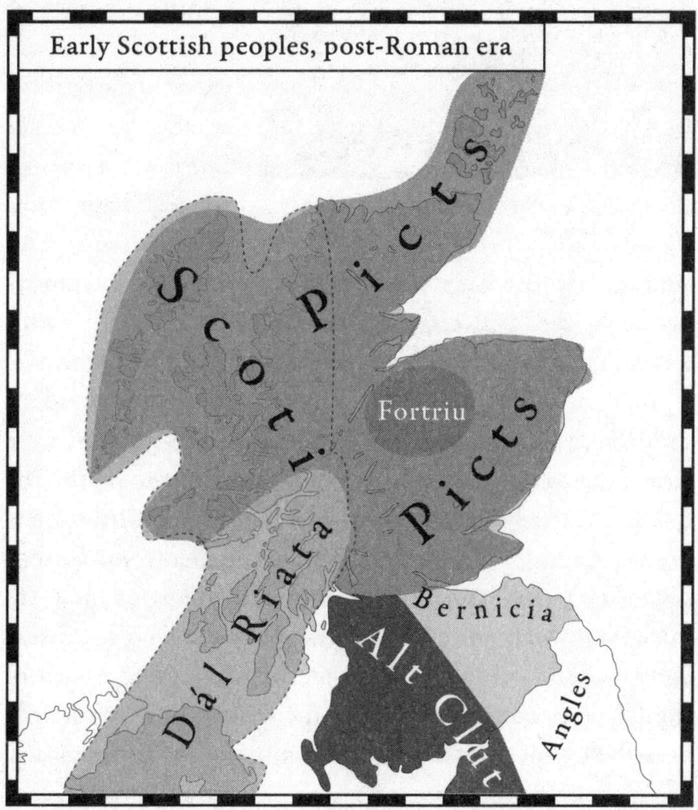

These were not the only post-Roman kingdoms in what would become Scotland. The Kingdom of Alt Clut (Strathclyde), with its chief stronghold at Dumbarton Rock, was in existence by 600. At its greatest extent, Alt Clut covered the western half of central Scotland and parts of the south-west into Cumbria, with a possible northern border at *Clach nam Breatann* (Rock of the Britons) at the far end of Loch Lomond, where Pictish, Scottish and Alt Clut lands all met. This kingdom of Strathclyde was thus uncomfortably sandwiched between the Scottish, Pictish and later Northumbrian realms, and was intermittently subject to all of them.

Dumbarton Rock and Castle. Detail from watercolour by Thomas Girtin, *c.* 1793

In 870 Dumbarton Rock was sacked by new invaders, the Vikings, at the same time as Wessex and its allies were struggling to fight off a huge Viking army in the south. The fall of Dumbarton, *Dùn Breatann*, Fort of the Britons, was probably a major disaster, since it was commented on by four sets of surviving Annals and Chronicles. Many of the fort's inhabitants were sold into slavery, and following the defeat the kingdom's strongpoint was moved to Govan, south of the Clyde in modern Glasgow. The kingdom of Strathclyde nonetheless survived in some form into the eleventh century.

The Columban Mission

Christianity was introduced into Scotland early in the post-Roman period. The Celtic saint known as Ninian (likely a misreading of 'Uinniau') is credited with evangelising the south-west of Scotland and parts of Fife and Angus in the sixth century AD, while St Columba (Colum Cílle), a nobleman of the Uí Néill (O'Neill) dynasty from the north of Ireland, founded a monastery on Iona in the 560s. From this tiny island in the Inner Hebrides, Columba and his successors carried a mission into central and northern Scotland. Their progress can be traced via today's place names. The presence of 'Cill' or 'Kil' as a Gaelic element indicates a historic church or burial ground, as in Kildonan, Kilmarnock or Kilsyth.

When Columba arrived on Iona, the island was part of the kingdom of Dál Riata and under the rule of Conall MacComgaill (r. 558–74). Indeed, King Conall may have personally invited the future saint. As we have seen, the north of the island of Ireland already formed part of the cultural Irish-Scottish world of the Gaelic-speaking westerly kingdoms of Scotland (Conall's successor, King Áedán, would rule in Ireland's North Antrim). Columba's biographer Adomnán, abbot of Iona from 679 to 704, records:

> In the vicinity of that part of Caledonia where St Columba chose to begin his new career, there is a cluster of isles known at the present day by the synonym of 'The Hebrides', which isles, or at least some of them, seem to have then been subject to the prince who ruled over the Scottish colony which had settled in Caledonia. The sequestered site of the present Hebrides admirably adapted them for the seclusion of the monastic life, and in such a retreat as they afforded, the saint felt convinced that the followers of his institute might devote

> themselves most freely to the holy exercises of the cloister. His connection with Conall, the sovereign of the above colony (for Conall, like Columba, was lineally descended from the Dalradian dynasty) gave reason to hope that he might obtain permission to found a monastery in one of these islands: he sought it and was successful; Hy, the smallest of them, now distinguished by the name of Icolmkille [Iona], being generously bestowed upon him by the prince for his use and that of his children in Christ. Taking twelve of these with him, Columba sailed from Ireland, and the weather proving propitious, all safely arrived at Hy of the Hebrides. The great things operated there for God deserve, and shall find place, in a new chapter.

Columba's monastic and religious leadership in Scotland was concentrated in the mainland and Hebridean islands of the west. However, the saint's high status as a nobleman of the Cénel Conaill, one of the great Irish dynasties, meant that he wielded extensive networking clout across the Scottish Gaelic world.

The faith Columba promoted was essentially that of the Catholic Church. It was not, despite some differences of opinion regarding monastic practices and the date of Easter, that of a distinct 'Celtic Christianity' imagined by later Protestants in search of historic roots. The so-called 'Celtic-Roman' controversy over the date of Easter was not a conflict between two separate Christian traditions, but between older and newer practices of the Catholic west.

The Columban mission was not Irish or Scottish in a modern national sense. It did, however, receive royal support, and in turn its increasingly influential hierarchy bolstered the standing of the Crown. There were still several centres of power in northern Britain, but over time Columba and his legacy helped consolidate that power in fewer hands. The main beneficiary was the emerging kingdom of the Scots, and later Scottish kings would adopt Columba as a symbol of royal legitimacy – and of the centrality of the Church to that legitimacy. From the beginning, Columba's mission had much common ground with the Scottish kingdom in the west, not least a shared language. Columba's biographer Adomnán claims the saint laid hands on Áedán MacGabráin at his accession to the kingdom of Dál Riata in 574, symbolising the unity of religious and secular powers.

This spiritual reinforcement would certainly have been welcome to Áedán. A volcanic eruption in AD 536 had caused demographic disruption throughout the northern hemisphere, cooling the climate by about 2 degrees Celsius and putting pressure on crops and population alike. Áedán repaid Columban confidence by ramping up his military activities, raiding as far as the remote Orkneys in 580, around Stirling in 582, and into Man and Ireland (where he may have asserted the independence of the Dál Riata Scots by rejecting a claim of overlordship by the Irish High King).

Columba himself – or the public memory of him in the Scottish kingdom – thus played a crucial part in establishing the basis for the supremacy of Gaelic-speaking Scotland and its crown. In time the Catholic Church would become, after the monarchy, the second most important institution of the new Scottish kingdom, integral to its culture and self-image.

Trouble from the South

For the moment, however, it was the Anglians of Northumbria (the historic north of what is now England) rather than the Church who made their presence felt in Scotland. Northumbria comprised two kingdoms: Bernicia in the north and Deira in the south (though Bernicia tended to dominate, with the Deiran king often subordinate to his counterpart). Bernicia was a sizeable territory, including not only the modern county of Northumberland but also the areas we know as County Durham, Tyne and Wear, Berwickshire and at times Lothian as far as the Pentland Hills. Deira was on the Yorkshire and Lincolnshire coasts, between the Humber and Tees rivers.

Northumbrian incursions affected Picts and Scots alike. In 603, Áedán was defeated by Aethelfrith of Bernicia at Degsastan, possibly in Liddesdale in what is now the Scottish Borders. By 640 the Northumbrians were laying siege to Dun Eidyn (Edinburgh), and not long afterwards Oswald of Bernicia (r. 642–70) and his family were harassing the Scots as far north as Stirlingshire. Oswald's kingdom reached at least from the Forth to the Tees, and by 681, Trumwine, a Northumbrian, had been consecrated 'bishop of the Picts' with his seat at Abercorn on the southern shore of the Forth west of Edinburgh.

By the late seventh century, this southern encroachment of military, political and religious power was beginning to look permanent. But in 685, Bridei III, King of Fortriu, or northern Pictland (r. 672–93), defeated an invading Northumbrian host under King Ecgfrith at 'Dunnichen' (Dun Nechtain), either at Dunnichen Hill, five kilometres east of Forfar, or at Dunachton, close to Kingussie. The former site is the traditional one and better fits the logistical requirements of an invading army, which would need to move along the strip of land between the mountains and the sea (from where it likely received supplies). Although the battle probably involved no more than 2,500 men, Bridei's victory over the Bernician invaders proved decisive. In the 680s the king is reported as ravaging as far as Orkney, and he may have been effective suzerain from Orkney to Forth and

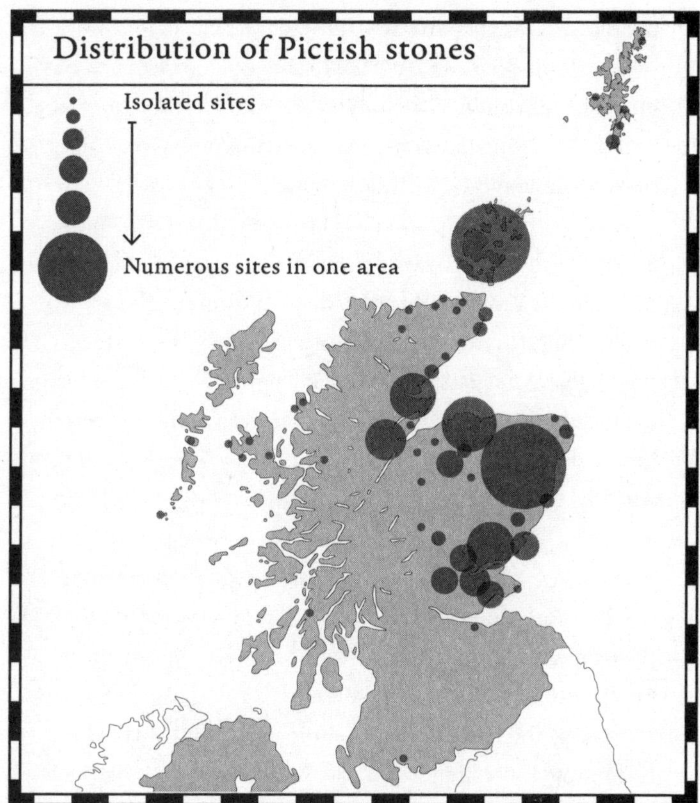

Buchan to Argyll. While Northumbrian rulers continued to challenge from the south, with Bernicia adding Kyle to its territory for a time after 750, they ceased to be a military threat north of Forth, Indeed, after some further struggles at the turn of the eighth century, a new frontier may have emerged in the area of the Pentland Hills, about ten kilometres south of Edinburgh.

Who Were the Picts?

It was the Romans who first gave the Picts their name – *Picti*, meaning painted ones – no later than the third century. They were long seen as a mysterious, vanished people, displaced by the Scots. Even as late as 1899, a work such as John Buchan's *No Man's Land* could present these one-time inhabitants of Scotland as a hidden and repressed part of the national self, enigmatic and unknown to science, but somehow surviving underground.

The Picts themselves were said to claim descent from the Scythians, nomadic warriors from the Eurasian steppe – but then the Scots would claim descent from the Egyptians and the English from the Trojans. In fact, like the Scots and the English, the Picts inhabited a recognisable early medieval society. They probably spoke a language akin to Welsh, in which they were called *Prydyn*. Placenames beginning with 'Aber' (Aberdeen, Abercorn, Aberfeldy) are clearly cognate with Welsh equivalents such as Aberystwyth.

The image of the Picts as a people of mystery owes something to the lack of written records. It also stems from a simplistic and racialised view of world history popular in the nineteenth century, with its fondness for narratives of total conquest (and total defeat / elimination). But there is no real sign that the kingdom of the Picts (or kingdoms: there may have been one as far north as Orkney) was anything other than one more emerging polity trying to centralise power – in broad terms, the successor of the federation led by the Caledonii that had proven so troublesome to Rome.

Fortriu, the core Pictish powerbase, is now believed to have been in the north and north-east of Scotland rather than in Perthshire and central Scotland, as used to be thought. If so, its legacy may perhaps be seen in the power of the *mormaír* or stewards of Moray (discussed later) in the early centuries of the unified Scottish kingdom.

The concept of a Pictish kingdom survived in the successor polity of Alba, later Scotland, whose rulers were known as

'Kings of the Picts and Scots' until the early tenth century. Soon after, however, the term 'Picts' seems to have died out.

Seaborne Scandinavians

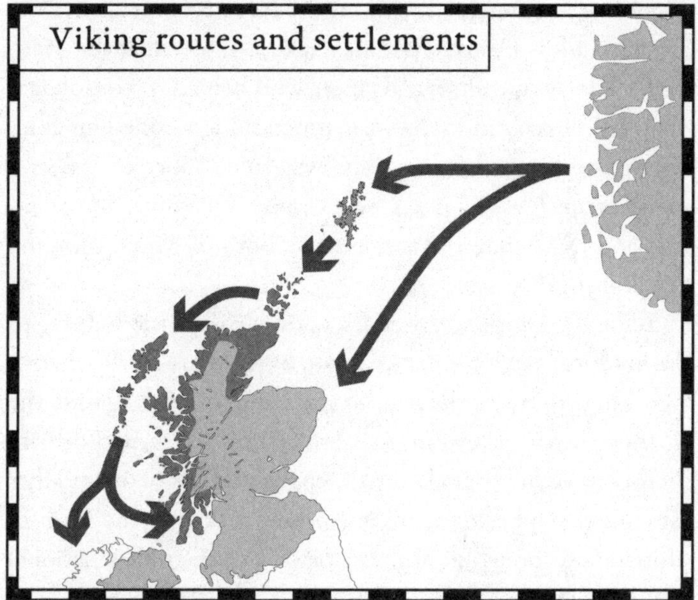

The *Anglo-Saxon Chronicle* places the first Viking – largely Danish – incursion into Northumbria at Lindisfarne in 793, and these seaborne Scandinavians likely made their presence felt in Scotland around the same time. By 800, Norwegians seem to have been established in the Hebrides and Shetland, while the Columban monastery on Iona to the west was burnt in 802. Not long afterwards, the Book of Kells, now in Trinity College Dublin, was moved from Iona to Ireland, probably to keep it safe. The Viking invaders forced Alt Clut and Dál Riata to move eastwards, though Pictish church settlements on the east coast also came under attack. Norse placenames can now be found from south-western Scotland to Shetland.

The First King?

Cináed MacAilpín (d. 858) is traditionally identified as the first King of Alba: the ruler who forged Dál Riata and the Pictish kingdom into a single unit occupying most of Scotland north of Forth–Clyde – albeit without the Norwegian west and the northern isles. Historians today take a more nuanced view, seeing him as one of several rulers who helped to consolidate what was already in many ways functioning as one kingdom. The territory that became Alba was ruled more or less as a whole at much earlier dates – by Unuist (Óengus I, r. 729/32–761) and by Causantín (r. 789–820), both of whom took the title King of Pictland.

Tellingly, Scotland owes its national flag, the Saltire, to the mythical tale of a prayer made by Óengus II, the Pictish high king, to St Andrew in 832, during a battle against the Northumbrian army at Athelstaneford in East Lothian. Victory was duly signalled to Óengus and his Scottish allies through the appearance of St Andrew's cross in the form of white clouds on a blue sky. The origins of the oldest national flag in Europe, commemorated at Athelstaneford's Flag Heritage Centre, thus reflect the importance of both the Picts and Scots to the country's history.

It may be a simplification to classify Cináed as the first king of a united Alba, but his family certainly dominated the early succession. He is also associated with a royal residence, still being excavated, at Forteviot in Strathearn near Perth, which remained a stronghold of the Scottish crown from the early ninth until at least the late eleventh century. Cináed was the son of a king of Dál Riata, and himself ruled there, as well as among the Picts. In Scotland as in England, the pressure of Viking raids in the west and the north spurred deeper political integration.

SCOTTISH PLACENAMES WITH NORSE ORIGINS

Place Name	Origin	Translation
Busby	Buskr + by	Bush village
Humbie	Hundr + by	Dog village
Eriskay	Eric's ey	Eric's Island
Scalpay	Skalp-ey	Boat-shaped Island
Westray	Vestr-ey	West Island
Jura	Djúr-ey	Deer Island
Kirkwall	Kirkjuvagr/Kirkevold	Church's Bay
Dingwall	Þingvöllr	Assembly field
Tongue	Tunga	Spit of land
Twatt	þveit	Clearing or paddock
Laxdale	Lax + dalr	Salmon valley
Seaforth	Fjörðr	Sea loch
Hestwall	Hestr	Horse field/wall

SCOTTISH WORDS WITH NORSE ORIGINS

Scots Word	Old Norse/Danish	Meaning
Greet	Græd	Cry
Een	Øjne	Eyes
Keek	Kigge	Look
Dook	Dykke	Dive
Bairn	Barn	Child
Ken	Kende	To know
Haar	Haar	Sea fog (mist/hair)
Flit	Flytte	Move/Flutter
Muckle	Meget	Much/Big
Reek	Røg	Smoke
Kilt	Kjalta	To tuck up
Scaff	Skaffa	To acquire
Hame	Hjem	Home

In 849, the arrival of another Viking host in the west prompted a further transfer of Columban relics and other precious items from Iona to the mainland and Ireland. The bones of the saint himself were relocated to Dunkeld. At this point, the king's court likely moved to the area round Perth. Cináed was simultaneously fighting the Northumbrians to the south, while his son Causantín or Constantine I, King of the Picts – the title was still in use – died fighting the Vikings in the Scottish heartland of Perthshire. It was not until his nephew Causantín Mac Áeda, Constantine II (r. 900–43), defeated the Vikings in Strathearn in 904 that the kingdom of Alba could begin to emerge more fully.

Everyday Life of the Picts and Scots

Today the 'Pit' placenames of Scotland are mostly found in the farming heartlands of the old Pictish kingdom in the east: Pitmedden near Aberdeen, Pittodrie in the city itself and Pittenweem in east Fife. The term often indicates a farm. Farming was dominated by dairy and cereals, and in both Pictland and Alba 'fermtouns' of a few houses grew up around the productive land. Oats appear to have been introduced in response to the damper and cooler conditions of the sixth century. The *dabach* (davoch) was a later measure, apparently denoting the area of farmland needed to fill a container with a single unit of tribute or obligatory payment to the landowner.

In Gaelic culture, lesser farmers owed tribute to their overlords, and food and hospitality to the local sub-king. Money was not used except in the form of bullion. The king could expect the support of his people in driving out unwelcome invaders, in the cultivation of crops and in practicing the Christian faith, but key features of a developed society such as currency and markets were absent, and would not be widespread in Scotland until the reign of David I in the twelfth century.

The Picts used red sandstone for the cross slabs on which they carved intricate designs and important scenes. These survive in locations such as Dunnichen and Portmahomack in Easter Ross, which appears to be the first Pictish monastic site, dating from *c.* 550, and possibly a major power centre within Fortriu.

Finds at Pictish and early Scottish sites bear witness to trade with the Mediterranean and the late Roman Empire. Amphorae have been discovered at Rhynie, and evidence of commercial exchange with Aquitaine has been found both at the Dál Riata stronghold Dunadd in Argyll and at Whithorn in Galloway. In everything from architecture to personal adornment, the influence of Frankish and Carolingian culture can be seen, though in general the impression is of a certain conservatism in design. This a recurrent theme in Scotland: for example, fortified houses continued to be built well into the seventeenth and eighteenth centuries, their purpose being to celebrate martial history rather than to offer a realistic mode of defence.

The Dawn of Alba

The title of 'King of the Picts' disappeared with Constantine II in the first half of the tenth century. Scotsmen now began to be identified as *Albannaich*, after the new kingdom of Alba. Anglo-Saxon sources recognised the shift, using the term 'Scottas' for the first time. It was an ambiguous term. The lands of the *Scoti* on both sides of the Irish Sea were still closely intertwined, and for the next two or three hundred years *Scoti* would be used indifferently to describe both Irish and Scots. (At this time the Irish were far more active throughout international Christendom, so foreigners who used the term tended to be referring to them rather than to the Scottish Scots.)

Irish culture permeated the kingdom of Alba. The person of St Columba represented the cultural and religious links between Ireland and the Scottish kingdom, and from the ninth to the eleventh centuries the spread of the Gaelic language at the expense of Pictish strengthened their linguistic kinship. There was literal kinship too: the royal houses were related by blood, with two of Constantine's uncles reigning as High Kings of Ireland.

The new kingdom of Alba was not identical to present-day Scotland. Its core was the Scottish mainland north of Forth–Clyde as far as the Great Glen between Inverness and Argyll. The islands in the west and north remained under Viking control while Northumbria still stretched into the Lothians. Alt Clut's successor, the post-870 kingdom of Strathclyde, continued to compete sporadically for power in the west-central mainland, at least as far south as Carlisle. Even so, Alba was developing into a secure and powerful kingdom with its own monarchical rituals. Mainly these were enacted in the southern Pictish areas, with the most important ceremonies being held on the Moot Hill, or Hill of Belief, near present-day Scone Palace. Constantine's coronation in 905–06 was the first we know of, the last being that of Charles II in 1651 (though one was planned for James 'VIII', the Jacobite claimant, in 1716).

The path to nationhood would, however, be a troubled one.

CHAPTER 2

THE STRUGGLE WITH ENGLAND

The English kingdom and the kingdom of Alba emerged at almost the same time. In what is now England, the victories of Alfred the Great, King of Wessex (r. 871–99), over the Danes, combined with the Danish evisceration of Northumbrian power, left the southern kingdom as unquestionably the senior player. By Alfred's reign, Wessex stretched from Oxfordshire to the south coast and from Kent and Essex to the Cornish frontier and beyond.

Alfred's successor Edward the Elder (r. 899–924) took substantial new territories back from the Danes and defended Northumbria from incursions by Causantín mac Áeda, or Constantine II. His work was expanded by Aethelstan (r. 924–39), who from 927 exercised West Saxon lordship over Northumbria, thus becoming substantively the first king of England. In 934, Aethelstan claimed himself to be *rex totius Britanniae*, king of all Britannia. Alba was on his mind, and he attacked in the same year, reaching as far as the Mounth on the east coast and laying siege to the stronghold of Dunnottar. By September 934, Aethelstan was back in Buckingham in the south of England, accompanied by Constantine, who had submitted to him as *subregulus*, sub-king. Eógan (Owain) of Strathclyde had also submitted. In 935, Constantine was first in the order of Aethelstan's sub-kings called to court at Cirencester. By the end of that year, though, he had returned to Scotland, where he set about planning revenge for his humiliation (as he may have seen it, for the kingdom of Alba had its own sub-kings).

To this end Constantine allied with Strathclyde and the Norse king of Dublin. A mighty conflict ensued in 937 at

Brunanburh (possibly Bromborough in the Wirral), when Aethelstan's army prevailed against 'the Scots people', as the Anglo-Saxons were now calling them. An elderly Constantine – now in his sixties if not seventies – was considerably weakened. In 943, he passed the crown to his cousin Máel Coluim mac Domnaill and retired to a religious house at Cennrígmonaid, modern St Andrews.

Battle of Brunanburh (illustration by Amédée Forestier)

St Andrews would play an increasingly important role in the affairs of the kingdom from around this time. The monastic centre was much enhanced there under David I (r. 1124–53). Encouraged by the king, in 1140 Bishop Robert founded a cathedral priory, with the aim of turning St Andrews into an archbishopric. Part of the growing Scottish resistance to the claimed overlordship of the English Church, this alarmed the Papacy, which tended to side with the English Crown in disputes between the two kingdoms.

Máel Coluim (Malcolm) I (r. 943–54) – the name means 'servant of Columba' in deference to the growing role of the Scottish Church in national consolidation – seems to have been determined to re-establish the power of Alba. It may have been during his reign that Strathclyde was dismembered, with Edmund of England (r. 939–46) taking the Cumbrian south – possibly in revenge for a revolt by the sub-king of Strathclyde – and Máel Coluim assuming overlordship of the north. As yet, though, these were not lasting settlements and the Strathclyde kingdom would survive, albeit in straitened form.

In 948–50, with fresh Danish attacks on York destabilising the Anglo-Saxons, Máel Coluim raided south as far as the Tees. The Scottish border was now approaching its modern configuration. Máel Coluim's son Cináed II (r. 971–95) prevailed in Lothian, repeatedly raided Northumbria, and in the 980s advanced as far as Cheshire. This was some years after he had met King Edgar (r. 959–75) to settle a boundary dispute there, an event later portrayed as a submission by pro-English sources. The plundering raid into Cheshire, like others of its kind, was typical of early medieval campaigning as carried out by kingdoms which had not yet acquired a bureaucracy or administration, but were in the process of emerging from warbands and small communities.

At the end of the first millennium, the distribution of power throughout these islands was in flux. Like his father before him, Cináed was killed in north-east Scotland, possibly in a squabble over the rules of succession, which he was alleged to have altered in favour of his own relations – that is, to a more modern concept of descent by blood. A few years later, in 1003, the Danish king Sveinn (Sweyn) Forkbeard (963–1014) attacked England with a raiding force. The previous November, Aethelred II (r. 978–1013; 1014–16) had ordered the genocide of all Danes in England; Sweyn's own sister had been killed in the massacre. By December 1013, Sweyn himself was king in England (also Norway) and reigned for the few weeks until his death in February the following year.

Aethelred fled to the Isle of Wight, where he nursed his ambitions for a return to the throne. He was not the only competitor for power across the islands. On 23 April 1014, Brian Boru, High King of Ireland (941–1014), narrowly defeated a combined force of Vikings and his Irish foes at Clontarf. In 1005, Brian had been credited with the title *'Imperator Scotorum'*, which some have interpreted as a claim to overlordship over the entire Gaelic world, in Ireland and Scotland. It has likewise been claimed that some of the lands in western Scotland paid him a form of tribute, but this is not confirmed by the sources. Borders and sovereignty remained slippery concepts as the first millennium drew to a close.

The Anglo-Saxon kingdom was now in a state of disintegration. Aethelred died in 1016, and his son Edmund Ironside was defeated in a Danish invasion led by Knútr (Canute). Edmund agreed to remain king in Wessex only, but the concession was moot as he too died shortly thereafter. Canute then ruled alone, and over the next few years also became King of Denmark and then Norway.

The Scots took advantage of the disruption. Máel Coluim II mac Cinaeda (Malcolm II, r. 1005–34) tried unsuccessfully to take Durham, but at Carham by the Tweed in 1018 he was victorious over the Northumbrians, helped by Eógan (Owain), King of Strathclyde and probably his sub-king. On the east coast, Northumbrian territory at times still ran up to 50 km into present-day Scotland. Canute's brother-in-law had been appointed Earl of Northumbria, but the Bernician north of that great earldom was ceded to the Scots after Carham, and a later invasion of Scotland in the early 1030s does not seem to have greatly changed the balance of power.

Around this time Máel Coluim also appears to have gained overlordship of Caithness and Orkney via his grandson Thorfinn Sigurdsson (*c.* 1009–65), who may have become a dependant at the Scottish court after the Battle of Clontarf. Although still far from being absorbed into the Scottish kingdom, Pictish-Scandinavian Orkney – whose authority at least sporadically reached the Oykel river in Sutherland, if not as far as Dingwall – was not always fully independent of it. By the twelfth century, the Earldom of Orkney was in any case semi-autonomous within the Norse polity, and indeed was a competitor for political influence in the Western Isles. Rather than being entirely Norse, Scottish or independent, the status of the earldom was triangulated somewhere between all three.

In 1039, King Donnchad (Duncan, r. 1034–40), Máel Coluim's grandson, made a disastrous intrusion into what remained of Northumbria. It may have been this that provoked Macbethad, *mormaer* of Moray and now better known as Macbeth, to challenge for the crown. The following year, Macbethad's forces defeated and killed Donnchad near Elgin, after which their leader became *Ard Rí*, High King of Alba. In 1052, when Earl Godwin of Wessex (*c.* 1001–53) called for the expulsion of Normans from England, Macbethad gave some of them sanctuary in Scotland. After a Northumbrian-supported challenge in Strathclyde in 1057, Macbethad was mortally wounded at Lumphanan in Aberdeenshire. Máel Coluim wrested the succession from Macbethad's stepson Lulach and in March 1058, he became undisputed king.

Máel Coluim III (r. 1058–93), while nominally submitting to the king of England, Edward the Confessor (r. 1042–66), was a highly effective and aggressive monarch. He attacked Northumbria in 1065 and over the next four years set about subduing Strathclyde. This was a response to West Saxon attempts to draw it into their orbit, and was successful – although the Lordship of Galloway remained semi-detached from the Scottish kingdom for almost another century. By 1070 the Anglo-Saxon monarchy had finally collapsed with the defeat at Hastings of Harold II (*c.* 1022–66), Earl Godwin's son, and the ascension to the throne of William of Normandy (r. 1066–87).

Edgar Aetheling (*c.* 1052–after 1125), heir to the Saxon throne, escaped with his family to Scotland in 1068. The next year, Máel Coluim supported Edgar in a Northumbrian revolt against William's rule, and seems to have attempted to impose Scottish overlordship to the Tees. In 1069–70, his forces reached into Yorkshire (Edgar Aetheling may have offered this land to the Scottish Crown in return for its aid). These invasions were unsuccessful, ending in a comprehensive Norman victory and the violent reprisals known as the 'Harrying of the North'. Edgar was left with few cards to play, though Máel Coluim appears to have taken the view that he and his family might rule all England in the unlikely event of a West Saxon restoration. He therefore married Edgar's sister Margaret in Dunfermline in 1070 on the site of the future abbey. Their first four sons were named Edward, Edmund, Aethelred and Edgar, all stout Anglo-Saxon names.

In the end, however, Máel Coluim's incessant raiding led to nothing more than the stronger and more secure integration of Northumberland into the English kingdom.

The king may have hoped that his son Donnchád by his late wife Ingibjorg Finnsdottir would rule in Scotland and that one of Margaret's sons would rule in England. Although this never happened, the marriage meant that the Scottish royal family were henceforward the legitimate heirs of the House of Wessex. Centuries later, this would play a role in bolstering the Stuarts' claim to the English throne.

St Margaret, Queen and Patroness of Scotland

Margaret long held the reputation of being a modernising and anglicising queen, but in reality matters were considerably more complicated. Despite her Saxon and cosmopolitan background, she was deeply interested in Scottish religious traditions. There was no doubt, however, that she was a transformative figure and was long and fondly remembered as such in pre-Reformation Scotland. She established a ferry across the Forth (remembered in the modern names of North and South Queensferry), supported consistent Catholic practices in the Church and served orphans and the poor, whose feet she washed, as well as bringing the Benedictines to Scotland. In July 1246, her great-grandson Alexander II (r. 1214–49) petitioned Pope Innocent IV for her canonisation, which was authorised in 1249 and celebrated at Dunfermline on 19 June 1250. Dunfermline Abbey became a shrine to Margaret and her husband, housing her venerated relics. Her head, which disappeared during the French Revolution, was

St Margaret's Chapel, Edinburgh Castle – stained glass of St Margaret

described as still having its golden auburn hair intact in 1785. Even in that era, Margaret was seen as a patron of patriotic Scotland. In 1693, her feast day was altered to 10 June so that it could be held on the same date as the birthday of the Jacobite claimant to the throne, the future James 'VIII'.

Feudal Scotland: Chiefs, Mormaír, Toísech ...

It was during these centuries that the internal contours of the modern Scottish kingdom took shape, with the beginnings of an organised regional administration of the king's justice. From the tenth century onwards, the *mormaír* (or great stewards) began to play a prominent role in regional leadership, acting alongside local judicial authorities.

The inaccessible geography of mountain and flood that made Scotland so difficult to conquer from the outside also made it tough to administer within. As a result, the Scottish Crown became more dependent than its English counterpart on regional magnates, who were theoretically – if not always practically – answerable to it. (It is worth pointing out that such figures were hardly unknown further south: take for instance the Percy family, who as Dukes of Northumberland challenged the English Crown into the fifteenth century.)

The terms *mormaer* (plural *mormaír*) and *toísech* are known to have been used in Scotland from the tenth century onwards, though they may pre-date this. It is possible they were engaged well before 900 as an instrument to incorporate the lesser kingdoms into the whole. This integration was by no means a smooth process, with the role of these 'stewards' sometimes becoming all but indistinguishable from that of a king, and indeed leading to claims of overlordship over all Alba (as with the *mormaír* of Moray). In the case of Moray, the title may have been used to downplay the status of its holders and clarify that they did not possess kingly authority. Although we don't know the precise role of the *mormaer*, it certainly encompassed both peacetime lordship and military leadership.

As a powerful representative of his region, the *mormaer*'s rise to office was influenced by local kindreds and their leaders, the *toísech* (though it was possible to hold both titles simultaneously). The *toísech clainne* was a leader of a kindred, and is sometimes also designated 'thane'. Geographical isolation, as well as the presence of competing power centres and disputes over marches and boundaries, tended to strengthen local relationships. Regional leaders had authority over tribute, aid, labour and military service as well as duties of hospitality to the Crown. The practical extent of their authority, and how independently they exercised it, was largely determined by the strength and perceived status of the current king.

In later centuries the powerful regional Scottish chiefs of the name of Campbell, Douglas, Erskine, Murray and others bear more than a passing resemblance to this early form of governance and leadership. The *mormaer* of Fife was not the only noble family to evolve into an earldom. From 1100 on, the great earldoms and lordships of Scotland (Angus, Argyll, Atholl, Buchan, Caithness, Carrick, Fife, Galloway, Lennox, Mar, Ross and others) blended forms of authority and jurisdiction deriving from both Gaelic and incoming traditions, often associated with the Franco-Norman knights who received land and offices under David I.

Major landowners might owe *caín* or tributary taxation to the king in return for the rights they exercised. Land grants were increasingly likely to be recorded as charters, rendering formal what had previously been a matter of custom. By the latter part of the twelfth century these rights could be inherited or married into, and some offices were heritable too.

Kinship relations were therefore central as the Crown drew an ever more close-knit nobility into its orbit, in an ever more formalised role. Despite later accounts of Máel Coluim III creating a range of aristocratic titles at his Forfar 'parliament', this had been a piecemeal process rather than a discrete event. Moreover, the term 'parliament' is somewhat flattering at this juncture: no parliament boasting anything more than advisory powers can be identified until the reign of Alexander II (r. 1214–49) – also the first king to use Royal Arms, which appeared on his Great Seal.

By the thirteenth century, 'justiciars' had been appointed for 'Scotia' north of Forth, Lothian and Galloway to exercise the judicial powers traditionally linked to the leadership of the *mormaír*. Government in Scotland was always mediated through a combination of institutions and aristocratic power, with the Crown generally striving to hold the latter within the limits of the former. Eventually, a single justiciar evolved into the role we know today as Lord Justice General or Lord President, Scotland's most senior lawyer. Beneath the justiciars came the sheriffs, who frequently inherited their office, and whose role as regional magnates was reflected in the division of Scotland into sheriffdoms. Regional sheriffdoms date from the early part of the reign of William the Lion (r. 1165–1214). By the close of the twelfth century all major landholders swore an oath to uphold the king's peace and justice.

Feudalism in Scotland concentrated administrative heft in the hands of powerful regional players. These great landholders might offer the king the service of a number of knights – or in the west, galleys – as military support in return for their lands. Known as 'ward holding', this form of tenure in return for military aid lasted until the Jacobite Rising of 1745. There were also forms of landholding for nominal service and for

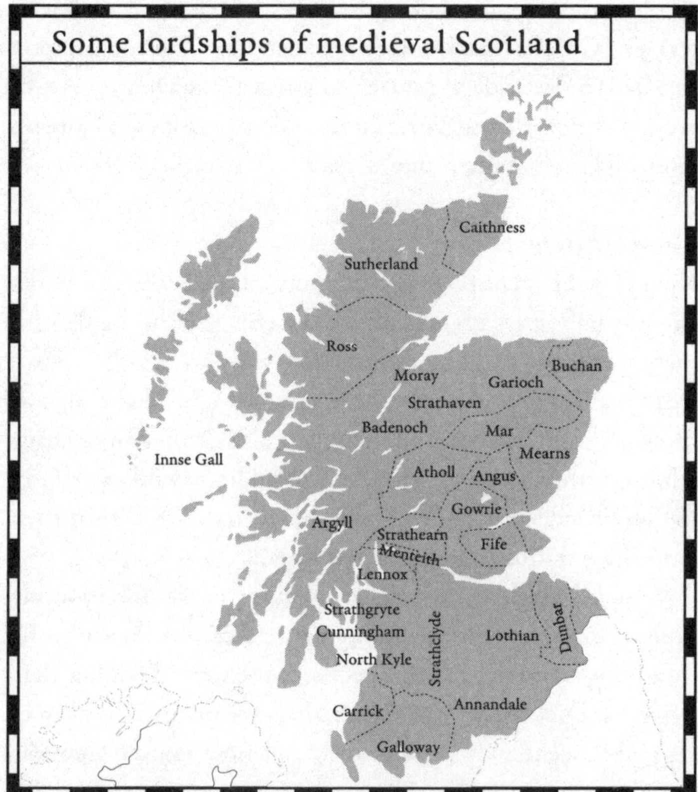

monetary obligation – *'feu ferme'* – where duty was paid to the superior by the vassal. Evolving from the earlier *caín* – tribute in kind to a superior, usually paid in food and livestock – feu duty survived until the close of the twentieth century, as did 'subinfeudation', whereby a new layer of feudal tenure could be created that extended the chain of obligation. In England, subinfeudation disappeared in the medieval period.

In Scotland's close-knit and highly interrelated society, with its strong and geographically separate regional power bases, aristocratic power was generally both feudal and kin-based in nature. The Duke of Atholl may have been one of the two or three greatest magnates of eighteenth-century Scotland, but he was also Chief of the Name (the paramount clan chief, a term also used in Ireland) of Murray, as surely as the Duke of Argyll was of Campbell and Lord Lovat – descendant of a Norman family – Chief of the Name of Fraser.

David I (r. 1124–53)

King David I spent huge capital sums on the Scottish Church (he was famously 'a sair sanct for the croun', meaning that his piety was a sore drain on the kingdom's resources). The Crown therefore had to find sources of revenue beyond what it already received from the regional magnates. To this end, David's administration came up with a new legal framework, establishing burghs who paid the Crown 'burgh ferme' rents for their embedded trading rights and privileges.

Like his predecessors, the king imported Franco-Norman knights into Scotland, thereby creating a cadre of nobles who owed their lands and rank directly to the Crown (rather than having acquired them in the traditional manner by way of regional ascendancy). These included now famous Scottish families such as Bruce, Fraser and Oliphant, as well as the Breton Walter FitzAlan, who became David's steward in 1136, and is the ancestor of the House of Stewart.

Flemings and Anglophone settlers from Scottish Lothian also settled in the burghs, expanding them and driving up trade. Aberdeen, Berwick, Dunfermline, Edinburgh, Elgin, Forres, Montrose, Perth, Roxburgh, St Andrews, Scone and Stirling all achieved early burgh status, and the privileged trading rights that accompanied it. Rather like the regional magnates, the burghs enjoyed powerful trading monopolies – Aberdeen's reached from the Cairngorms north to Banff and south to the North Esk, a distance of 120 km north to south, and 80 km inland – or almost half the size of Wales. Burgesses, the senior business class in the burgh, had a right to use the town's markets without paying tax and to hold land – 'burgage' – free of feudal overlordship. Their own courts oversaw internal disputes, while ecclesiastical centres of power also migrated to the burghs. In 1131, for example, the Bishopric of Aberdeen moved into the city from Mortlach in the countryside.

Despite the growing burghs, Scotland's population – at this time somewhere between a quarter and half a million – remained largely rural. There were still marked differences in regional trading identities, with Galloway looking west to Ireland and the islands, and the east-coast burghs towards Scandinavia and the Baltic coast. In the previous century, held back by the lack of a developed coinage, overseas trade had consisted mainly of pearls, animals and their products, and slaves (in particular women and girls, acquired during raids). By the 1140s, thanks to his control of the Alston silver mine in the Tyneside area, King David had enough bullion to introduce Scotland's first regular coinage.

King David's silver pennies literally promoted his image, underlining the sovereignty, unity and continuity of the monarchy. The king widened the royal prerogative in other ways too – for instance, by expanding the royal forests on the Norman model. In these areas, hunting rights were reserved to the Crown, though they were normally extended by grace and favour to the nobility. Everyone else was excluded, with savage penalties for poaching (though they were even more savage in England).

On the coast, many rural Scots lived in stone and turf chaumers (single-roomed houses), perhaps unchanged for thousands of years. Others in the fermtouns lived in wattle and daub or wooden buildings, now usually rectangular rather than round. Living space was shared with livestock. Farmers used oxen to plough and planted oats and barley, paying a duty to the landlord in food or fighting time. The land itself was divided into the better infield and the poorer outfield terrain, with cultivable ground divided into narrow rigs 200 metres long – a single run of the plough. This agricultural arrangement would last into the nineteenth century and the adoption of better-quality ploughs. Rigs had ditches between them – useful for courting couples – and their ownership might not be contiguous, so the owner of rigs A and C would have to defend his neighbour's, B, in order to defend his own.

Common grazing and other shared rights were the norm, and generally local craftsmen supplied the equipment and infrastructure necessary to the rural economy. Such roads as existed were of beaten earth and muddily impassable in winter. Not all settlements were connected by road – though there were a few *via regia* (royal roads), probably laid with the help of tributary labour. The south of the kingdom was more urbanised, but there is scant evidence of any north-south cultural divide at this time – between, say, the Black Isle and the Borders. The 'Highlands' is always an imprecise term and often a misleading one.

The acquisition of the rich farmlands of Lothian from Northumbria was a major boon to the Scottish kingdom. Arable cultivation spread in the southern uplands and commercial forestry expanded. Between 950 and 1250 in particular, the warmer climate of medieval Europe enhanced Scotland's marginal land. By 1290, Fife, the Lothians, Angus and Aberdeen were ranked roughly on a par with Winchester in terms of their ability to pay papal tithes (church taxes); and the west of Scotland was ranked higher than the bishoprics of Lichfield or Exeter. By the fourteenth century, the warm period would be

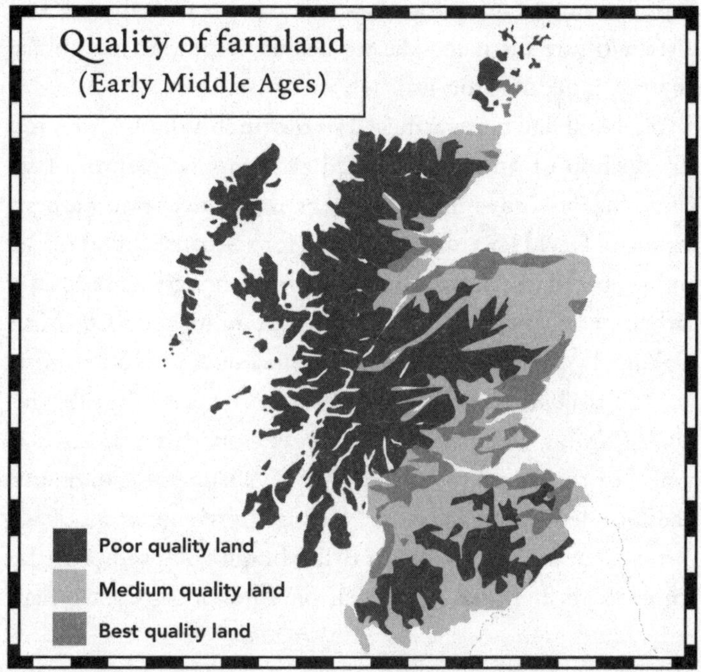

over and all of northern Europe hit by multiple harvest failures – but for now turf and stone farmhouses sprang up. At one point Kelso Abbey, which sits 300 metres above sea level, had over 100 hectares of farmland under cultivation, while viniculture was not unknown in the south of the kingdom.

With the arrival of Franco-Norman knights in the country came the motte and bailey castle. These characteristic Norman fortresses consisted of a wooden or stone fortified tower (the 'keep') on high ground (the 'motte', often called 'Castlehill' in placenames), surrounded by a walled or palisaded courtyard (the 'bailey'). An outer ditch or moat surrounded the whole. Several of the Scottish Normans were granted lands in the north (the great Gaelic earldoms of Fife, Mar and Strathearn also gained territory). One of the new landowners, Robert de

Brus, became first Lord of Annandale in 1124. In the not too distant future his namesake would play a central role in the Scottish kingdom's survival.

Scotland had never acquired its own archbishopric, and the Archbishop of York still claimed ecclesiastical control of its Church. The Crown increasingly resisted this claim. Early in his reign, David I pressed the papacy for a Scottish archdiocese, and prepared St Andrews to be its seat (though work on the cathedral only began in 1158 in the reign of his successor Máel Coluim IV (r. 1153–65)). The religious house at Dunfermline became an abbey in 1128, as did Kelso. In 1135, after the subjugation of Moray, a Benedictine priory was founded near Elgin as a sign of triumphal royal authority (William the Conqueror had founded Battle Abbey at Hastings from similar motives). Other abbeys at Jedburgh and Dryburgh followed. On the whole the bishops were more reliable allies of the Crown than

Melrose Abbey: print by William Simpson after J.M.W. Turner

the great nobility, and David's lavish spending on the Church in Scotland helped keep them that way. Continental religious orders now began to arrive in greater volume: Cistercians and others joined the Benedictines, who had been at Dunfermline since 1070. In 1136, Glasgow Cathedral was dedicated and Melrose Abbey was founded and colonised from Rievaulx in Yorkshire, whose abbot was a former Crown servant of David's. In the north, the archbishopric of Trondheim, founded in 1152, was limited in its jurisdiction to Orkney and the Hebrides, David now having secured effective authority over the Scottish mainland, with the possible exception of the north-east of Caithness.

David also planned to develop Carlisle Cathedral (the city was then in his lands) and even harboured an ambition to take York by force and integrate its archbishopric into Scotland. This grandiose dream came to nothing, and it was David's grandson William I (r. 1165–1214) who finally secured a new status for Scotland as a 'special daughter' of the papacy in 1192 – though it still lacked its own archbishop.

> Naturally it distresses you greatly, it distresses us also, that our dearest son Henry, illustrious King of the English, has compelled you to swear to obey the English church, since this reflects injury toward God and contempt for us ... And we have heedfully warned the aforesaid king ... We therefore command your fraternity and enjoin that you attempt not to obey by metropolitan right any but the Roman pontiff ...
>
> Pope Alexander III to the bishops of Scotland, 1176

The Holy See in Rome, having begun with asserting direct control over the Glasgow bishopric (which in its turn occasionally pretended to ecclesiastical authority in England as late as the 1260s), now assumed direct authority over all the bishoprics of St Andrews, Glasgow, Aberdeen, Brechin, Dunblane, Dunkeld, Moray and Ross & Caithness, leaving only Galloway under English episcopal overlordship, from which it eventually emerged only in 1355.

Scottish Identity

The Kingdom of Scots ruled by David was not a single people with an inherited community of culture, kin and law – and did not describe itself as such. There was a clerical unity based on St Columba, whose staff or crozier *Cathbuaid* was carried before Constantine's army as early as 918, and whose relic was also probably present at Bannockburn in 1314. The roles of Columba, Church and Crown were intertwined, and this triple alliance – as we shall see in the next chapter – would play a vital role in the political crisis that faced Scotland after 1290. A prayer to the saint from the reign of Alexander I (r. 1107–24) calls on 'Holy Columba, our father, born of mother Ireland' (an interesting admission of the Irish origins of the Scots) to 'be for the Scots a two-edged sword … a mighty rampart' and to 'increase King Alexander's virtue'. It enjoins the king to 'shape his royal acts according to the rule of law, for when the king is ruled by law, the realm is kept from harm.' In his turn Alexander II (r. 1214–49) was called 'Church's shield, people's peace, leader of the wretched'.

Monymusk Reliquary, long (and probably wrongly) identified as the reliquary of St Columba

Who were these people in the king's peace? The multinational nature of the kingdom was recognised in the early charters issued by David I, which mention Scots, Flemings, French, Galwegians and English. By the end of the reign of his grandson William I (r. 1165–1214), official documents have largely ceased to identify the inhabitants of Scotland by their ethno-cultural background. By the time of Alexander III (r. 1249–86), it is clear that there was increasing sensitivity to land owned by foreigners not domiciled in Scotland, with English absentee landholding coming under pressure.

Seannachie recites the royal genealogy at the coronation of Alexander III. From a manuscript of the *Scotichronicon* by Walter Bower

The Kingdom of the Scots had moved a long way from its Irish roots, although the links remained. Scotland's Stone of Destiny, on which its kings were inaugurated, was alleged to be hewn from the same rock as its Irish equivalent at Tara, seat of the High Kings. (In fact it was quarried no more than 50 km from Scone.) It wasn't only the Stone's fictional geological kinship that spoke of the kingdom's Gaelic foundations: they could also be seen in the role of the *seanchaidh*, the Seannachie or bard who recited the royal genealogy when a king came to the throne.

In the past some historians divided Scotland into Celtic and Germanic ethnic zones, in the 'Highlands' and 'Lowlands' respectively. In practice the Gaelic language was spoken from

Sutherland to the Lothians in King David's time, with early Middle English confined to the Lothians. There were also some speakers of Cymric (close to Welsh) in the southern uplands, and Norse was current in the far north and its islands. To further complicate matters, in addition to the four main tongues there were three minority languages: French (spoken at court), Flemish (in the burghs) and Latin (among clergy and educated laity).

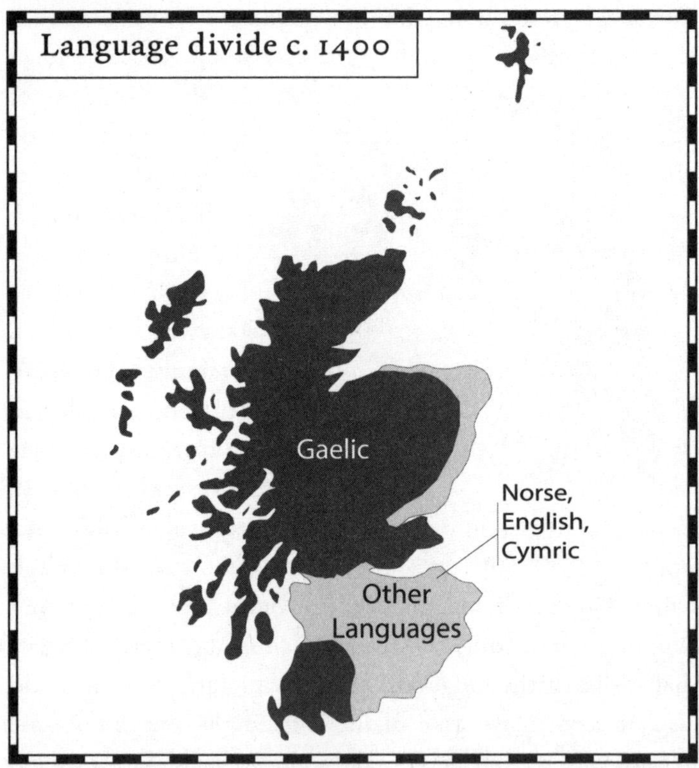

The prominence of Flemings and Anglophone Lothian Scots in the eastern burghs helped to promote the spread of Early Middle English, which evolved under the influence of Norse, French and Latin into what became the Scots language. By the twelfth century English-speaking had already spread to the west, and while in 1400 Gaelic was still seen as the language of the Scottish kingdom, a century later it had already begun to be identified with Ireland. 'Scots' was the name now given to the northern Anglic tongue. The language was widely adopted by speakers of Gaelic, and bilingualism was extensive. It is a historical fallacy to confuse language with ethnicity in Scotland. Even great Gaelic noblemen such as MacDougall of Lorne wrote in French when conducting court business, and by the early modern period it was not uncommon for ordinary 'clansmen' to be literate in Scots or English. There was no mystic Celtic identity: just lords and chiefs engaged in very worldly power plays from their more or less mountainous domains.

Strife with England

King David took an active part in politics in the south of the island, supporting his cousin the Empress Matilda (1102–67) against King Stephen (r. 1135–54) in the twelfth-century English civil war. Máel Coluim's granddaughter was now Holy Roman Empress, crowned in St Peter's in Rome in 1116. Matilda thus held the greatest title in Europe after that of the Roman Emperor in Constantinople, even if it was in her husband's right. Scotland was now a kingdom with family and diplomatic connections at the highest levels in Europe.

After invading Northumberland on Matilda's behalf, David had his son Henry installed as Earl of Northumberland in 1139. This was in the midst of his own triumphs over the English strongholds of Bamburgh, Clitheroe, Norham and Wark, his aim being to control England as far as York. By 1146 Lancaster was firmly in Scottish hands, and David's power stretched from castles as far north as Wick to an English city 125 km south of the current border.

It was not long before the Scottish kingdom's gains were lost. David may have overreached, but arguably he was as much the victim of ill luck in his old age as he had been favoured by fortune in the early years of his reign, when he'd been able to take advantage of a divided England. The death of his son, Earl Henry, in 1152 marked the beginning of a spectacular collapse. David died the following year in his mid sixties, leaving his grandson as king. When the teenaged Máel Coluim IV (r. 1153–65) tried to come to an agreement with the English king at Chester over his Northumbrian territories, his opposite number was not Stephen but his powerful successor, Henry II (r. 1154–89), founder of the House of Plantagenet.

Henry turned out to be far too tough a proposition for Máel Coluim. He demanded the return of all English lands to the English Crown, offering the Earldom of Huntingdon – a long way from the border, and a title which would involve vassalage to the English Crown – as a face-saving exchange. Máel Coluim was forced to accept.

Máel Coluim IV's reign was a turbulent one for Scotland. In the west the Norse–Gaelic warlord Somairle Mac Gilla Brigte (Somerled) (d. 1164), Lord of Argyll, Kintyre and Lorne, took up arms against his wife's father, the King of Man and the Isles, and pushed his dynasty out of both places. Then Somerled turned his attention towards the Kingdom of the Scots itself. In 1164, with Irish allies, he attacked the lands of Walter, now High Stewart (Steward) of Scotland. This was a step too far, and he was killed at the Battle of Renfrew, near modern Glasgow. After this fight, the title of High Stewart became hereditary to Walter's heirs.

Máel Coluim died in 1165. He was succeeded by his brother William, the Lion, who instantly set about trying to recover the Northumbrian territories. This project ended in disaster when he was captured in 1174 (the day after King Henry II had done penance for authorising the murder of Thomas a Becket). William thus became the first reigning Scottish king to be taken as a prisoner by England. Henry extracted full advantage from the situation, forcing William to accept the terms of the Treaty of Falaise. This stipulated William's formal submission to him, and ceded five castles in the Borders, Edinburgh and Stirling (in the event, Scotland did not formally become a fief, and only three castles were actually handed over). Henry also insisted on the continuing autonomy of the Lordship of Galloway (a perennial thorn in the side of the Scottish Crown) and forced William to marry Ermengarde de Beaumont, an illegitimate descendant of Henry I. This was certainly intended as an insult, part of the Plantagenet campaign to erode the status of the Scottish royal family. Later, injury was added to insult when the daughters of the union were married to English earls rather than being allowed to forge international alliances.

The English king Richard I (r. 1189–99) overturned most of the humiliating terms of Falaise in return for a large payment from the Scots to support his participation in the Third Crusade. Richard even offered the Scottish king Northumberland – without its castles. William rejected this obvious move to bring him under the greater influence of the English Crown: the gift would have effectively rendered him an English feudal landowner, without the infrastructure to contest the power of the English Crown in his 'own' land.

England's say in the marriage destinies of his daughters may have narrowed his foreign policy options, but within his own kingdom William was once again able to prosper. By 1202, he had permanently secured his position in Caithness in the north; and in 1209 what may have been the first free trade agreement with England bore witness to the growing commercial activities of the Scottish realm.

William's position was greatly strengthened by the support of major nobles, whose extensive lands in Scotland, England and France gave them options as vassals. Ironically, the weakness of the Crown tended to make these nobles more inclined to support it. Men such as Saer de Quincy, Earl of Winchester, Lord of Leuchars and Seneschal of Vaudreuil (1155–1219), could throw their weight behind the king of Scotland – the weakest of the three kingdoms in which they held titles – because that very weakness gave them more room to manoeuvre. Their support for the Scottish Crown left them freer to pursue their own ambitions and exercise their own authority unhindered in their Scottish lands. As time went on, this greater freedom of manoeuvre within a more decentralised kingdom helped turn many of the Scottish nobility into Scottish patriots, opposed to English rule out of self as well as national interest.

The last years of William's reign were marred by a struggle with England, possibly prompted by the offer of one of his daughters in marriage to the King of France. In the ensuing wrangle with King John (r. 1199–1216), his daughters Isabella and Margaret were taken hostage by the English. William's increasing perceived dependence on Scoto-French noblemen also caused resentment among the native elites at home, and in 1211–12 helped trigger a rising against his rule, which he needed John's help to curb. Military aid came at a price: William was forced to yield to the English king rights over the choice of bride for his fourteen-year-old heir, Prince Alexander.

John's growing problems with the papacy and with his own barons relieved the pressure on the Scottish king. Although William never regained either Cumbria or Northumberland, by the time of his death in 1214 – at the age of seventy-one and after almost fifty years on the throne – the achievements of his grandfather David had been significantly consolidated.

The political crisis brewing in England tested the mettle of the boy Alexander II (r. 1214–49), and the new king responded with vigour. He crushed dynastic rivals at home before taking advantage of King John's struggle with his barons to invade England on 19 October 1215 – though not before he had first held a 'parliament' or council in Edinburgh at which Alan of Galloway was re-appointed Constable of Scotland, bringing Galloway closer to the Scottish Crown.

On his way south, Alexander burnt Carlisle and Newcastle, going on to receive submission not only from Northumberland but also (in January 1216) Yorkshire. Hampered by the state of his kingdom, John was able to muster only a feeble counterattack. Alexander's Scottish army was able to reach Canterbury and, in late summer 1216, Dover. It was the furthest advance of any Scottish force into England at any time in the history of the two kingdoms.

At Dover, Alexander paid homage for his Northumbrian lands to the future King Louis VIII of France, who had invaded England in May from the south-east and was briefly proclaimed king by rebel barons in London. But the French and the Scottish invasions both proved shortlived. After John's death on 19 October, the English barons rallied behind the new king, Henry III (r. 1216–72). With the French army defeated at Lincoln, Dover and Sandwich, Alexander was forced to make terms. In 1221, he married Henry's sister Joan. If this bound him to England's dynasty, at least it did so at a level recognising his own sovereign royalty, with a bride of similar rank.

In 1237, the centuries-old Scottish claim over Northumberland was finally laid to rest by the Quitclaim of York. This fixed the Scottish border at its present position between the Solway Firth and the mouth of the Tweed (give or take a few square kilometres on its western side and the inclusion of Berwick in the Scottish kingdom in the east). It is the oldest agreed land border between European states still in existence.

The Nation Takes Shape

In 1218, Pope Honorius III had re-emphasised Scotland's position as a 'special daughter' of the papacy. Though Alexander's did not succeed in gaining papal authorisation for his being crowned with unction as an imperial sovereign, he and Henry III were treated as 'kings on equal terms' in the negotiations at York, and Alexander received a small land grant of property in Cumberland, Westmorland and Northumberland, with an annual rental of £200.

After Queen Joan's death in 1238, however, relations between England and Scotland deteriorated, not least because the following year Alexander married Marie de Coucy, scion of one of the greatest noble houses in France. The marriage renewed ties between the two countries: the networks that would underpin the formal 'Auld Alliance' half a century later were already evolving. In 1252, Alexander II's son Alexander III (r. 1249–86) incorporated a French emblem, the *fleur-de-lys*, in his seal, in recognition of his descent from Louis VI (r. 1108–37).

With Northumbria out of the picture, Alexander turned his attentions towards his realm's western periphery. In 1244, he tried unsuccessfully to buy the Hebrides from Norway. Two decades later, in 1263, his son Alexander III (r. 1249–86) narrowly defeated the Norwegian army at Langs in a chaotic but much-mythologised engagement. With the Treaty of Perth (1266), he finally secured the inner Hebrides and Man from Norway, in return for a small sum (which was never paid). With the exception of its outer islands, the Scotland we know today was taking shape.

The Great Seal of Alexander III, showing the *fleur-de-lys* on the throne uprights

Alexander III and his nobility continued to forge links with France. In 1270, Louis IX's (r. 1226–70) crusade against Tunisia was supported by Robert V de Brus (Bruce), Hugh de Bailleul (Balliol) and other members of the Balliol family, as well as the Earls of Atholl, Carrick and Dunbar, among others. In 1285, King Alexander married Yolande de Dreux (1263–1330), daughter of Count Robert IV and – like her husband – a linear descendant of Louis VI. Alexander's literally breakneck ride through a storm along the dark Fife coast to reach her bed the next year would end in his death. Seldom has a mid-life crisis – the heirless king was forty-four, his bride twenty-three – had such unfortunate political consequences (see next chapter).

In 1250, Margaret, Queen Consort of Máel Coluim III and 'Pearl of Scotland', was canonised, reinforcing the unity of Church and Crown that Columba long embodied. Now Scotland had both a royal and a clerical saint, a woman and a man, symbolically combining diversity and oneness.

The country might be a 'special daughter', but the papacy refrained from settling the question of the Scottish Crown's full sovereignty. Scotland was not a dependent or a client kingdom – but neither was it an imperial state, sovereign in all respects. In pursuit of this latter status, Alexander II had applied to Rome to be 'anointed and crowned' in 1233, but was refused due to English pressure. Alexander III was similarly unsuccessful, though in 1251 the Pope did deny the English king any authority over the Scottish rite of coronation. When he paid homage to Edward I of England at Westminster in 1278, the Scottish king was careful to specify that, though he owed fealty to the English Crown for 'the lands which I hold of you in the kingdom of England', his own kingdom was a different matter:

> To homage for my kingdom of Scotland, no one has right save God alone.

The cathedral dedicated to Scotland's foundational saint, Andrew, was not yet an archbishopric, but by 1279 its bishop's seal bore the image of St Andrew crucified, and in 1286 it also appeared on the seal of the Guardians of the Kingdom, accompanied by the legend 'Andrew be leader of the compatriot Scots'.

From multiple kingdoms to a kingdom with multiple peoples to a single Scottish nation, the journey of the Kingdom of Scots seemed complete.

CHAPTER 3

CRISIS, RECOVERY, DECLINE

Quhen Alexander our kynge was dede,
That Scotland lede in lauch and le,
Away was sons of alle and brede
Off wyne and wax, of gamyn and gle.
Our golde was changit into lede.
Christ, borne in virgynyte,
Succour Scotlande, and ramede
That stade is in perplexite.

When Alexander our king was dead
Who as leader gave Scotland shelter and law and order
Abundance of ale and bread were gone
Of wine, beeswax and rent, of sport and enjoyment.
Our gold was changed into lead.
Christ, born of a virgin
Help, support and cure Scotland
Placed among such manifold difficulties

Early fourteenth-century Scottish song,
recorded in Wyntoun's *Chronicle*

The War of Independence

At the time of his fatal tumble in 1286, Alexander III was in desperate need of a male heir. In the event, his granddaughter Margaret, daughter of King Erik II of Norway (r. 1280–99), was the only candidate for the throne.

The Maid of Norway was only three years old when she became queen in 1286, and never made it to Scotland during her short reign. With no effective ruler, the Scottish nobility chose seven regents or 'Guardians of the Community of the Realm' from their number: two earls, two barons and three bishops (one of whom, the Bishop of Dunkeld, himself died not long after taking office).

Scottish nobles with holdings in England were placed in an awkward position. Without a king of their own, the fealty they owed to Edward I of England (r. 1272–1307) for their estates on the southern side of the border weighed heavily on their decisions. When the infant Margaret became queen, the Guardians arranged a dynastic union between her and Edward's son, reserving Scotland's right in future to be an independent kingdom with its own institutions, customs and laws.

Margaret died on her first voyage to Scotland in 1290. Edward seized the Isle of Man for England and held a parliament in Norham in 1291 where he proclaimed himself overlord of Scotland. As king-maker he adjudicated between the thirteen competitors now vying for the Scottish Crown, finally coming down in favour of the French-born John de Bailleul (John Balliol, 1249–1314, r. 1292–6) against the rival claim of Robert V de Brus (Robert Bruce the Competitor, c. 1215-95). Both were descended from the same grandson of David I. Balliol became King of Scots on St Andrew's Day, 30 November 1292.

The Auld Alliance

Edward tried to keep the new King of Scots in his place with a series of petty humiliations. The Scottish nobility, treated as feudal vassals of the English king, eventually bridled at the prospect of being sent as auxiliaries to fight the French. In July 1295, a Scottish delegation negotiated a treaty of mutual defence with France, which also committed King John's son in marriage to the King of France's niece. This pact, which stipulated that if either country was attacked by England, the other would invade English territory, marks the start of the 'Auld Alliance'.

The Auld Alliance was never formally revoked, though it would be seriously weakened by the Scottish Reformation and was effectively ended by the 1789 revolution in France. As much a cultural as a political alliance in later ages, inspiring everything from architecture to poetry, it is still remembered nostalgically today.

In English eyes the treaty with France was tantamount to an invitation to war. Edward responded rapidly, invading Scotland and sacking Berwick with the trademark brutality that would earn him the nickname 'Hammer of the Scots'. The Scottish army was defeated. at Dunbar. John submitted to Edward at Montrose on 8 July 1296, and two days later at Brechin he abdicated his throne.

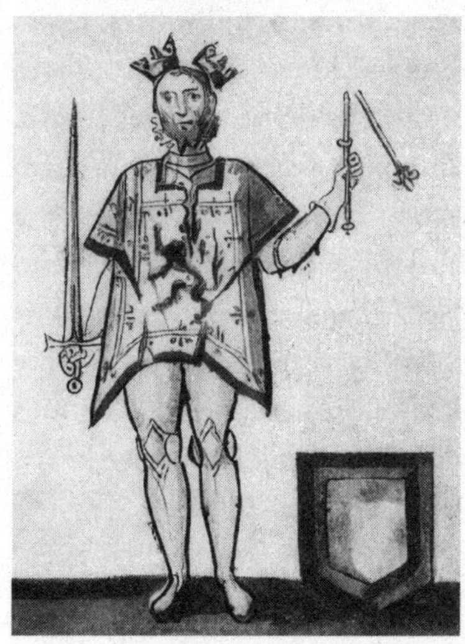

King John with an empty coat of arms and a symbolically broken crown and sceptre (from the Forman Armorial *c.* 1562)

King John's brief reign had been a disaster. He had failed to defend his realm, let alone extend it. Unable to administer justice at home independently of the lordship of an English king, he had been equally powerless to pursue his own foreign or military policy. He was altogether shorn of the attributes necessary for a medieval king. Stripped of his royal authority, physical and spiritual, he would be known to posterity as 'Toom Tabard' (meaning 'Empty Coat') – 'all fur coat and nae knickers' as today's colourful Scots phrase would put it. After his deposition, John lived comfortably on his estates in France, showing little interest in returning to fight for his crown alongside those still loyal to him. In time his son – whom he had ingratiatingly named Edward – would attempt to destroy the kingdom built by his successor, Robert VII de Brus (1274–1329), better known today as Robert the Bruce.

English Attempt Takeover

By the time Edward went on campaign to France in August 1297, taking a number of Scottish nobles with him, Scotland was becoming unruly. In the absence of a Scottish king, Edward had appointed the Earl of Surrey, who in turn devolved his authority to a supporting cast including Walter Amersham as chancellor and Hugh Cressingham as treasurer. The infamous 'Ragman Roll' of 1296 required all other landowners across Scotland to show fealty to the English king.

Nine of the twelve Scottish bishops refused the 1296 oath. In the west, Robert Wishart, Bishop of Glasgow, and William Lamberton, Bishop of St Andrews, together with Walter the Stewart and Robert VII de Brus, set aside their differences to rally against the English takeover. 'I must join my own people and the nation in which I was born,' de Brus is reported to have said, putting the common cause ahead of his personal ambitions for the Scottish throne – something that would not always be the case in the wars that followed.

Early Victories

Scottish resistance quickly gathered momentum. In May 1297, William Wallace (1270/2–1305), a landholder and vassal of Walter the Stewart, killed the English Sheriff of Lanark. In the same month Andrew de Moray, nephew of one of the former

Guardians of the realm, Sir John Comyn Lord of Badenoch, raised the standard of resistance at Ormond Castle in the Black Isle. His forces swiftly overran the English garrisons at Inverness, Moray and Banff. By summer, De Moray's army had taken back all Scotland north of the Spey.

In an attempt to stall an English retaliation, de Brus, the Stewart and Bishop Wishart pretended to negotiate while secretly helping Wallace to raise an army. In July, Cressingham reported to London that it was impossible to raise taxes, since the English were confined to their strongholds. Still playing for time, de Brus and the other nobles formally submitted to England that month, while in all probability continuing to support Wallace and de Moray, whose forces had rendezvoused at Dundee.

Moving to face the threat, the Earl of Surrey led an English army of several thousand men up to the River Forth. Confident the Scots would not contest his heavy cavalry and men at arms, on 11 September he began to move his troops across the narrow bridge at Stirling. High above him in the ruins of an Iron Age hill fort on the Abbey Craig, where the Wallace Monument now stands, Wallace and de Moray took up their position. The land of mountain and flood was about to come to the fore once more.

When enough of Surrey's forces had crossed the river, the Scots generals ordered an infantry charge from the higher ground. It was one of the earliest and most famous recorded uses of the schiltron, or Scottish pike phalanx, and the English army was cut in two. Many of the heavily armoured troops were pushed into the river and drowned. Although De Moray was badly – as it turned out, mortally – wounded, the English defeat became a rout. As Surrey retreated, Walter the Stewart and the Earl of Lennox harried his fleeing forces. Cressingham – who would normally have expected to be ransomed, given his rank – was killed and skinned in a vicious piece of theatrical symbolism: to Scottish eyes he had been 'skinning' Scotland through taxation. To ram home the metaphor, Wallace is said to have had some of Cressingham's hide made into a purse. In a subsequent attack into Northumberland, Wallace was again triumphant and became Guardian of Scotland.

English Fightback

Edward couldn't accept this humiliation. He raised an army of as many as 26,000 men, including more than a hundred noblemen and their vassals and many longbowmen from his recent Welsh conquests. On 22 July 1298 at Falkirk, the English heavy cavalry drove off the Scots archers and, though Edward's horse could not break the schiltrons, his archers could. As the Scottish numbers thinned, the English cavalry charged through the gaps. Both sides suffered heavy casualties but the Scots were outnumbered almost three to one – the outcome was an overwhelming defeat. Wallace soon resigned his Guardianship. At Stirling, the Scots had both mountain and flood on their side. At Falkirk, they had neither. Giving battle without the formidable advantages of terrain was then – as so often – fraught with risk.

Despite his enormous army, Edward still did not control the country north of Forth–Clyde, which remained in the hands of the Guardians until 1303. That year the French made terms of peace with England that excluded the Scots. Robert VII de Brus had already made his peace with Edward when the English king marched north in 1303, taking Scots strongholds. In February the next year, his commanders defeated Wallace at Happrew in the Borders. The former Guardian of Scotland fled to his final redoubt in Selkirk Forest. Edward held a parliament in St Andrews in March before taking the last major holdout in Scotland, Stirling Castle.

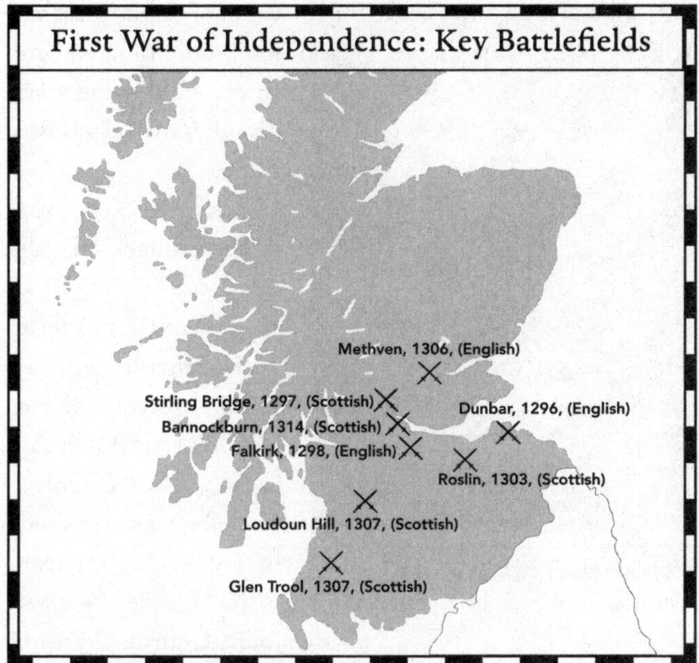

Defeat, Subjection – and a New King

Scotland was no longer a kingdom. Its nobles were now expected to swear allegiance to Edward as their direct overlord. Most did, though a few, like the exiled Guardian John de Soulis, held out. Wallace made a last attack in Perthshire in late 1304, then spent months on the run before being handed over by Sir John Menteith to be tried as a traitor by an English king to whom he had never owed allegiance. He was hanged, drawn and quartered at Smithfield on 23 August 1305, possibly as part of London's Bartholomew Fair entertainments. The next month, Edward made arrangements to govern Scotland as a province in the manner of Ireland, run by English nobles and collaborating Scots. He had already removed Scotland's archives, regalia and signs of sovereignty and Crown status such as the Black

The Stone of Scone within the Coronation Chair at Westminster Abbey (*c.* 1875–1885)

Rood of St Margaret and the Stone of Scone. The latter would spend seven centuries in Westminster Abbey.

Meanwhile, in 1304, de Brus, though officially in Edward's peace (i.e. an apparently willing subject of the English king) had struck a secret alliance with Bishop Lamberton of St Andrews. Only a few obstacles remained to block Robert's path to the throne. One was John Comyn, Lord of Badenoch, who after Wallace's execution was the strongest supporter of the king-in-exile, John Balliol. Initially Comyn came to terms of a sort with de Brus, but soon the two fell out. On 10 February 1306, they came to blows. De Brus stabbed Comyn in front of the altar of Greyfriars Kirk in Dumfries before his supporters finished him off. On 25 March, de Brus was crowned King Robert of Scots.

Less than a third of Scotland's nobility supported King Robert. The Comyns, including the Earl of Buchan, cousin to the man he had killed, were furious. Other powerful nobles such as John Comyn's uncle, Alastair MacDougall, Lord of Argyll and Lorne, backed their cause. Robert's kingship looked doomed.

The infighting suited an ageing Edward, who arranged to have the new Scots king excommunicated by Pope Clement V.

Edward's new Scottish commander Sir Aymer de Valence, later Earl of Pembroke, marched north. De Brus achieved some limited military successes, but his forces were soon outweighed by de Valence's heavy cavalry, which overran the Scottish army in a dusk attack at Methven, while MacDougall defeated them again at Dalrigh near Tyndrum. King Robert found himself isolated in central Scotland. His wife and daughters were captured by English troops and treated badly: his sister Mary was hung in a cage from the walls of Roxburgh Castle.

That winter de Brus fled to Rathlin Island in the Irish Sea, and then hid in Ireland, or possibly South Uist – the later legend of the spider in the cave is set around this time. Early in the spring of 1307 he landed with a small group of followers at Turnberry in Ayrshire, now home to a Donald Trump golf resort. Another group led by two of his brothers landed further south, only to be defeated by MacDougall's forces. Almost at once, de Brus was on the run again.

In April, the tide began to turn. King Robert's men ambushed and defeated an English force at Glen Trool. Then, on 10 May 1307, despite being outnumbered perhaps five to one, they won a resounding victory against de Valence at Loudoun Hill. Using tactics reminiscent of Stirling, the Scots dug a series of complex earthworks to protect their schiltrons from the English cavalry sent to mow them down. The English knights struggled to breach the Scottish defences and their horses lost their footing on the uneven and boggy ground. The Scottish pikemen them emerged to finish the task. It was de Brus's first major military triumph as king.

Marching north to relieve his troops, Edward I fell ill, probably of dysentery, and died on 7 July. Although his son Edward II (r. 1307–27) continued his father's invasion and received the submission of some Scottish nobles, his forces made little progress against Robert's guerrilla tactics and he soon returned south again.

Scotland's new king set about securing his realm by first quelling all opposition from within. On 23 May 1308, despite once again finding himself outnumbered four to one, Robert I defeated the Comyn forces at Oldmeldrum near Aberdeen, going on to destroy their power base in the '*herschip*' (harrying) of Buchan. The Earl of Ross submitted and Aberdeen surrendered. Later that summer, at the Pass of Brander in Lorne, the king defeated the MacDougall army by sending his archers up the steep mountainside of Ben Cruachan to rain down death from above. With small, highly manoeuvrable armies and unpredictable tactics, King Robert was now winning victory after victory: he knew how to protect and move his slower pike phalanxes, how to use his nimble bowmen for ambush and surprise, and how to deploy his limited cavalry resources to nullify the enemy's advantage in archers.

It was Scotland's good fortune to have a king who was also an outstanding general. By the end of 1308, Robert had won back enough land to set up an effective civil administration and to begin issuing government acts in the name of the Scottish Crown. Although Edinburgh and Stirling castles, together with other fortresses across the Borders, were still in English hands, it was becoming increasingly difficult to supply these northerly outposts. Edward II invaded again in 1310–11 but only reached the Forth–Clyde area. His army was harried all the way by the Scots, who revenged themselves further with a deep strike south on Durham in 1312.

Despite his victories, Robert I generally preferred to be bought off rather than putting soldiers in the field. The north of England was gradually impoverished as he extracted many times the taxes these counties already owed to the English exchequer.

The king also slighted many castles in Scotland after recapturing them, deliberately damaging their defences so they could not be used as enemy strongholds in the future. In 1312–13, Robert seized Dundee and Perth and regained the Isle of Man. His troops took Edinburgh Castle in a surprise attack and slighted it afterwards, leaving only St Margaret's Chapel unharmed. On Shrove Tuesday 1314, Robert's general Sir James Douglas (1286–1330) overcame Jedburgh, with Roxburgh following soon afterwards. Sir James was one of the outstanding military commanders of the era, long known as 'the Black Douglas' in England because of the terror he inspired.

Bannock Burn

There was still one obstacle to final victory, the great crag-top castle at Stirling. Robert's brother Edward had reached an agreement with Sir Philip Moubray, the English commander at Stirling, to surrender the fortress unless an English army came to its relief by midsummer 1314. Scotland's fate hung in the balance. If such an army came, the Scots faced the prospect of a pitched battle and the reversal of all their recent gains.

And such an army did come. Edward II brought 15,000 men and 2,000–3,000 armoured horse. On good ground, little could resist the charge of English heavy cavalry at speed. By comparison King Robert, who commanded the Scots in person, had four brigades – four schiltrons – of pikemen, around 6,000 in all, and 500 mainly light cavalry. The Earl of Moray's brigade stood to the front, close by Stirling Castle, with Edward de Brus and Walter the Stewart and their men behind, the latter commanded by Sir James Douglas. The king's personal command stood at the rear. The English approach was hampered by pits and caltrops – iron stars that project a spike whichever way they land – prepared by King Robert's men.

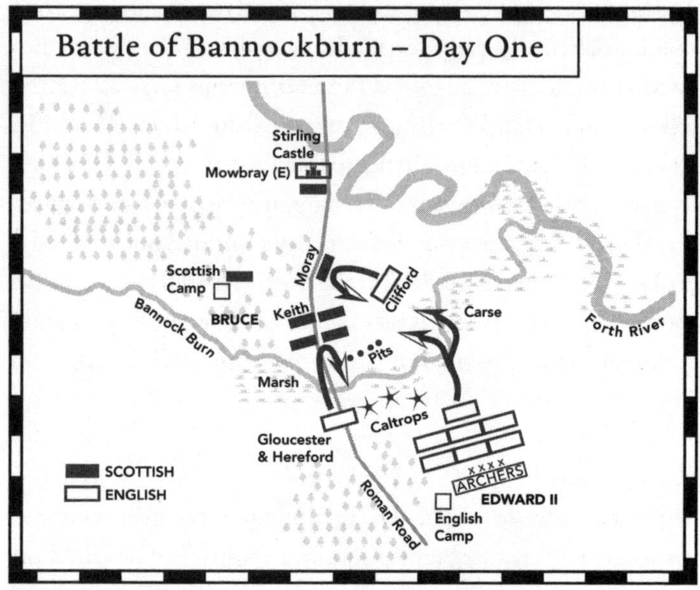
Battle of Bannockburn – Day One
Stirling Castle
Mowbray (E)
Scottish Camp
BRUCE
Moray
Keith
Clifford
Carse
Forth River
Bannock Burn
Pits
Marsh
Caltrops
Gloucester & Hereford
ARCHERS
EDWARD II
English Camp
Roman Road
SCOTTISH
ENGLISH

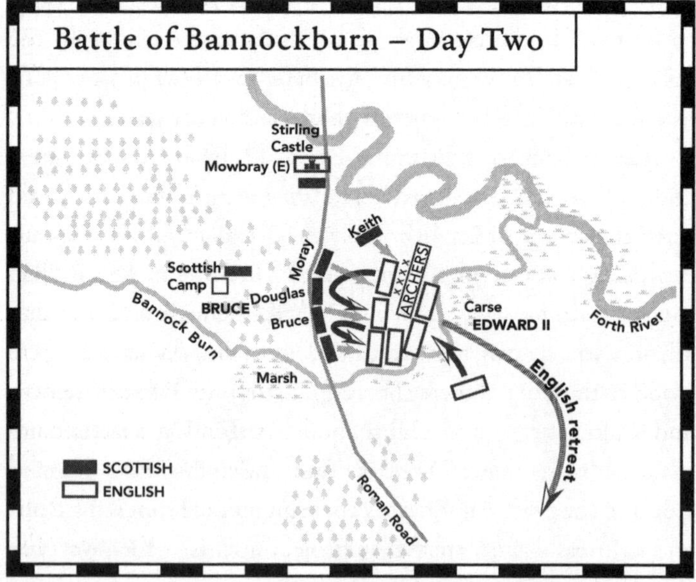
Battle of Bannockburn – Day Two
Stirling Castle
Mowbray (E)
Keith
Moray
Scottish Camp
BRUCE
Douglas
Bruce
ARCHERS
Carse
EDWARD II
Forth River
Bannock Burn
Marsh
English retreat
Roman Road
SCOTTISH
ENGLISH

The Earls of Gloucester and Hereford led the English vanguard. On 23 June they made a cavalry charge across the Bannock Burn, a stream some three kilometres from the castle, with the aim of decoying the Scots away from an attempt by Sir Robert Clifford and Sir Henry Beaumont to reach the castle. No doubt they also hoped to break up the Scottish force, or at least weaken its will to resist. But the booby-trapped ground broke their charge. King Robert killed Hereford's nephew, Sir Henry de Bohun, in full view of the combatants. Meanwhile Moray's brigade held off the attempted relief of Stirling.

The Scottish king was still considering withdrawing from a full-scale battle, but intelligence from Alexander Seton, who came over to the Scots from the English army, changed his mind. Bernard de Linton, Abbot of Arbroath, was by Robert's side and the two men invoked the saints of the Scottish nation to stand by its people. On the morning of 24 June, the armies faced each other by the Bannock Burn – Edward de Brus to the fore, followed by Moray, then Douglas and the king's own command. The Scots were outnumbered three to one. Once again Gloucester's heavy cavalry attacked, smashing into the leading schiltron, but the pikemen held firm. Gloucester died on the Scottish spears.

Robert's army began to advance, pushing at the disorganised English troops. As at Falkirk, Welsh and English archers shot into the exposed Scottish flanks, but King Robert ordered Sir Robert Keith, Marischal of Scotland, to charge them with his cavalry. With no major combat arm to protect them, the archers were swept away. King Robert then committed his infantry reserve under Aonghus Óg MacDhomnuill (Angus Og MacDonald, Chief of the Name of Donald) and under this extra press of spears the English army started to disintegrate. From King Robert's command post on the hunting forest site of Coxet Hill, lightly armed Scots and camp followers now streamed down towards the English army, reportedly calling *'On thaim on thaim on thaim thai faile!'* ('Attack, attack, attack, they are failing'). A general flight and panic followed. King Edward escaped capture by the skin of his teeth but Hereford was taken, to be exchanged for King Robert's queen, his daughter and his sister. The Bannock Burn was choked with the bodies of the less noble or fortunate. Water and rising ground had once again helped the Scots. The feudal host of England was utterly defeated.

Despite this crushing blow, Edward II still refused to recognise Scotland's independence. King Robert's leading commander Sir James 'the Black' Douglas continued the war, sacking Hartlepool in 1315. More daringly still, Robert enlisted Irish support through his links by marriage to the Earls of Ulster. On 2 May 1316, his brother Edward de Brus was crowned *Ard Rí*, High King of all Ireland, near Dundalk. As he was heir presumptive to the Scottish throne, this opened up the possibility of a united Irish–Scottish polity – and he may have been planning to become overlord of Wales too. In 1317, King Edward de Brus marched south to drive the English out of Dublin, but quarrels between Irish leaders hampered his progress. He was defeated and killed the next year, just when he seemed on the brink of forming a functioning government. King Robert continued to maintain a degree of Scottish power in Antrim and Down in the north of Ireland until the end of his reign, but the grand ambition to redesign the political future of the British Isles died with his brother Edward in 1318.

Final Battles

In that same year, Berwick fell to the Scots, followed by the capture or isolation of Carlisle, Norham and Newcastle. Edward II's army of 10,000 men was humiliated, Scottish forces pushing them back to the Trent. A truce gave way to a further attack from

Scotland on the northern counties. Then Edward's forces briefly invaded Scotland but were pushed out. At Byland near York in 1322, King Robert, Sir James Douglas and the Earl of Moray destroyed the English army under the Earl of Richmond.

The ensuing truce held for five years. On 4 August 1327, the English army under its new king Edward III (r. 1327–77) was defeated at Stanhope in Weardale when, to cries of 'Douglas! Douglas! Die my English masters!' Scottish heavy cavalry under Sir James overran the English camp in a night attack reminiscent of de Valence's at Methven twenty years before. King Edward's chaplain, members of his household and his staff were all cut to pieces before the army – now bolstered by mercenary soldiers from abroad – could rally to defend the English king.

At last King Robert had got what he wanted. Scotland's formal and complete independence was recognised at the Treaty of Edinburgh of 17 March 1328. The treaty was ratified in Northampton on 4 May. (England did not return the Stone of Scone as agreed, though after many adventures it is now the centrepiece of a new museum in Perth.) Pope John XXII had already recognised Robert's title in 1324, and in 1326 the alliance with France was renewed under the terms of the Treaty of Corbeil.

King Robert died on 7 June 1329, just before a final posthumous victory. Six days after his death, the Pope granted permission for the King of Scotland to be crowned and anointed by a papal representative. This divinely recognised sovereign right put the Scottish Crown shoulder-to-shoulder with the great European monarchies and placed it within a tradition going back to King David of Israel. Just over a year later, the king's heart was carried into battle by Sir James Douglas against the Moors of Granada. A monument now stands at Teba in the province of Málaga, where Sir James and other Scottish crusading knights were killed on 25 August 1330.

Freedom Is a Noble Thing!

The Scottish historian Abbot Walter Bower (1385–1449) attributed to Wallace's uncle the proverbial advice, 'Never submit to live my son / in the bonds of slavery entwined'. A similar sentiment dominates Archdeacon John Barbour's (*c.* 1320–95) epic poem *The Brus*:

A! Fredome is a noble thing!	Ah, freedom is a noble thing!
Fredome mays man to haiff liking.	Freedom appeals to human beings
Fredome all solace to man giffis,	Freedom gives them solace
He levys at es that frely levys!	They live at ease who live freely

Barbour goes on to link the victory at Bannockburn to the 'small folk', noting that the 'symple yumanry' can be 'as good as a knight'. He thus tied the nobleman Robert de Brus to the popular national cause associated with William Wallace. To be born a Scot of any rank was to be free – 'A Man's a Man for a That', as Barbour's successor Robert Burns, the great Romantic poet of personal and sexual liberation, would put it in 1795. It was highly effective rhetoric, but it wasn't only rhetoric.

King Robert's tomb in Dunfermline Abbey reads '*Hic jacet invictus Robertus Rex benedictus ... ad libertatem perduxit per probitatem regnum scottorum*' ('Here lies blessed and unconquered King Robert ... by probity he led the Kingdom of the Scots to liberty'). Another epitaph describes him as 'the nation's virtue ... a Paris ... a Hector ... royal rose of soldiery ... a Socrates, Maro [Vergil] or Cato in his words ... beloved as the Macedonian [Alexander the Great], like Arthur a jewel among men, a leader of the peoples, a Maccabaeus for intelligence'. It goes on in the same vein for stanza after stanza before exalting the king as a sacrament, 'sating men's hearts with sweetness, he was their holy food'. Many of his contemporaries knew the truth: without Robert VII de Brus, Robert I of Scotland, the Scottish nation might not have survived.

If force of arms, generalship, statesmanship and strategy were needed to deliver Scotland's freedom, so too was a highly developed propaganda war. Propaganda is a constant throughout history, though it takes many different forms. In the medieval period, propagandists typically focused on a king's rights of ancestry and descent. Geoffrey of Monmouth (*c.* 1090/1100–*c.* 1155) popularised what was to become the English foundation myth in his *History of the Kings of Britain* (1136), which traced the English Crown back to the mythical Brutus of Troy, great-grandson of the Trojan hero Aeneas and a descendant of Noah. In the story, Brutus came to the British islands and there had three sons. Locrinus became king of England, Kamber ruler of Wales and Albanactus chief of Scotland. As the eldest, Locrinus had authority over the other two, and so – by implication – did his descendants.

In the Scottish version of this myth, Brutus and Albanactus were brothers and shared sovereignty as equals, but it was not noted by the English chronicler. Instead, the Scots, Picts and Irish became the opponents of King Arthur in his unfolding story. The monks of Glastonbury Abbey conveniently 'found' King Arthur's tomb in 1191 to promote their abbey and underwrite the reputation and legitimacy of the House of Plantagenet. Edward I of England was the inheritor of this tall tale, and its widespread adoption might have warned the Scots elite of the risk posed by Plantagenet ambitions north of the border.

There was another Scottish counter-narrative, in which Scota, daughter of Pharaoh, brought Jacob's Pillow (see Genesis 28) first to Ireland and then Scotland – the famous Stone of Destiny housed at Scone. But this origin story was a poor relation to Geoffrey's 'Matter of Britain', as his propaganda came to be known. What the Scots developed instead between the 1290s and the 1320s was a far more sophisticated understanding of nationhood and the whole question of freedom.

The Declaration of Arbroath (6 April 1320)

Littere directe ad dominum Supremum Pontificem per communitatem Scocie

[Letter to the Supreme Pontiff by the community of the Scots]

The 'Tyninghame' copy of the Declaration of Arbroath

But from these countless evils we have been set free, by the help of Him Who though He afflicts yet heals and restores, by our most tireless Prince, King and Lord, the Lord Robert ... like another Maccabeus or Joshua ... Him, too, divine providence, his right of succession according

> to our laws and customs which we shall maintain to the death, and the due consent and assent of us all have made our Prince and King.
>
> Yet if he should give up what he has begun, and agree to make us or our kingdom subject to the King of England or the English, we should exert ourselves at once to drive him out as our enemy and a subverter of his own rights and ours, and make some other man who was well able to defend us our King; for, as long as but a hundred of us remain alive, never will we on any conditions be brought under English rule.
>
> It is in truth not for glory, nor riches, nor honours that we are fighting, but for freedom – for that alone, which no honest man gives up but with life itself.

The Letter to the Pope from the Community of the Realm of Scotland or the *Declaration of Arbroath*, as it came to be known, was probably drafted by Bernard de Linton, Abbot of Arbroath and King Robert's Chancellor. It explicitly connected the identity of the Scottish people with the independence of their kingdom, and had its roots in the repeated attempts made by Scotland to have its full secular and ecclesiastical sovereignty recognised by the Papacy.

But there is also perhaps a deeper influence, deriving from one of the greatest philosophers of the West: the Blessed John Duns Scotus (1265-1308), Professor at the University of Paris. A Scot from the border country of Berwickshire, frequently fought over by the rival kingdoms across the centuries, Scotus became a key philosopher of personal and political freedom. In his writing on civil authority, he set out the basis of what he considered to be legitimate political authority.

Duns Scotus (portrait from the series of Illustrious Men of the Studiolo of the Duke in the Ducal Palace of Urbino, 1308)

1. Social Contract: the people are to choose their ruler by agreeing among themselves as to who the ruler should be.
2. The people also choose the principle of transference of authority. This is crucial. It is not that the people choose the first ruler, and that thereafter the question of who is to rule is out of their hands; on Scotus's scheme, it is never out of their hands.
3. The ruler is put in place because there is a job to be done, one that requires exercise of practical right reason (i.e. prudence). Scotus argues that the ruler must be able to guide the people better than the people individually can guide themselves.
4. The people can choose as a ruler either a single person or a 'community'.

Scotus' conclusions are exactly consonant with the political outlook of the Arbroath letter, which is more socially inclusive than it is often given credit for.

There were two major allusions to these ideals within Arbroath itself, the first monarchical and the second republican. The first was the document's reference to Joshua (Hoshua Ben Nun), the leader of the Israelites after Moses, and more significantly to Judas Maccabeus (191–160 BC), whose defensive warfare had done so much to affirm the status of the Jewish kingdom in the second century BC. Indeed, the use of the term 'nation' as a statement of identity is first found on Maccabean coinage. The Declaration spoke the language of nationhood deriving from Israel and also showed both that the Scots had 'historic regnal unity' and that they had the 'right to independence', a right historically defended by the Community of the Realm of Scotland. As Arbroath made plain, this extended beyond barons and freeholders to a non-defined group that lay beyond and socially below these leaders of the community (and elsewhere defined as modest freeholders or even burgesses).

This takes us to the second important allusion in Arbroath. The appeal to liberty in the Declaration derives from the letter of a plebeian in the Roman Republican writer Sallust's *Bellum Catilinae* (*Catiline's Revolt*). Arbroath quotes these words almost directly in speaking of the 'liberty alone, which no good man loses unless with life itself'. The 'good man' of both Sallust and Arbroath is no baron, no member of the equestrian order or senator, but a common member of the plebeian people of Rome or Scotland. In other words, the Scottish nation is far more than its barons. The Declaration famously states that if King Robert should act against the interests of the Scottish nation, then the political community can – following Scotus – replace him as king.

The Declaration was sent in the names of eight earls, the High Stewart, Edward Keith (the future Marischal) and more than thirty other nobles, a greater number of nobility than those who guaranteed Magna Carta in England. The names include the Earls of Fife, Lennox, Moray, Orkney, Ross and Sutherland – the entire geographical reach of Scotland.

Like Magna Carta, the popularity of the Declaration has waxed and waned over the centuries according to the political climate. 'Tartan Day', first celebrated in Nova Scotia in 1987 and extended across the United States by Resolution 155 in 1998, goes so far as to link Arbroath to the American Declaration of Independence. Clause 1 reads:

> Whereas April 6 has a special significance for all Americans, and especially those Americans of Scottish descent, because the Declaration of Arbroath, the Scottish Declaration of Independence, was signed on April 6, 1320 and the American Declaration of Independence was modelled on that inspirational document.

The evidence for the claim is slim, if suggestive: the Scottish-American James Wilson (1742–98) was one among the first generation of leading patriots to appear to quote the 1320 Declaration directly. What is not in doubt is that Arbroath is one of the earliest – if not *the* earliest – statements of national self-determination in Europe. Years of bloody conflict and struggles against the odds had made Scots think deeply about their nation, its nature and its claims to exist. The resulting document presents the case for a Scottish national polity in a way that was and remains transformative.

William Wallace's last word was not 'Freedom', as *Braveheart* (1995) would have it, but the film bore witness to a fundamental truth of the Scottish cause, upheld not only by the cosmopolitan John Duns Scotus (whose epitaph reads 'Scotland bore me, England sustained me, France taught me, Cologne holds me') but by the humblest pikeman who triumphed before Stirling Castle in midsummer 1314.

The Lives of Scots at Home and Abroad

Who were these Scots, and what was their country like under King Robert and his successors? There were up to a million people in medieval Scotland, though the population was curtailed by the poor harvests of the early fourteenth century and then devastated by the Black Death of 1349–50. Scottish land became increasingly marginal in the wetter, colder European climate. Rising import costs, not least of grain, led to the effective devaluation of the currency after 1367. The English pound rose in value from 2 Scots merks in 1373 to 3 in 1390. The exchange rate was 4.5 merks by the 1450s, an era traditionally seen as a golden age for southern English agriculture and real wages.

In the time of Robert I, there were already eighty-six religious houses in Scotland, including thirty abbeys. From the fourteenth century, the growing number of endowed churches and religious houses became became ever more burdensome for a country with shrinking productive land. The problem was compounded after 1500 by rapid food price inflation. Between 1550 and 1585 alone, there were twenty-six bad harvests.

The financial strain placed by the medieval Church on Scottish society is frequently overlooked as a source of widespread support for the Reformation. Parish resources were all too often diverted to cathedrals, collegiate churches, abbeys, monasteries and universities. On the other hand, the alliance between Church and Crown was the keystone of the Scottish nation, enduring from Columba to the Wars of Independence via King David's pursuit of clerical independence. When one institution foundered, the other would be seriously damaged, as we shall see.

Intensive livestock farming was a feature of rural society in Scotland. Cattle were commonly moved between summer and winter pastures – larger flocks of sheep, often held by religious houses, might number up to 12,000. Wheat, oats and bere barley were the main crops. Along with kale, cheese and mutton, these were the staples of the Scottish diet. Many ordinary folk were deficient in iron and there was high infant mortality. As in most medieval societies, things were different for the upper echelons: at Prince David's wedding in 1328, for example, porpoise and sturgeon were served. Yet some misfortunes affected all. Leprosy was endemic and bubonic plague was a not infrequent and brutal visitor.

From such thin data as we have, it looks as if health may have been better in the countryside than the burghs, where between half and three-fifths of burials were of children under six. Feral animals helped to spread disease, there was no public sanitation and dietary deficiencies are evidenced by loss of tooth enamel and bone damage. In some places, leprosy may have affected as many as 20–25 per cent of the population. The crowded world of the town remained a natural home for plague and other pandemics as late as the seventeenth century.

The growth of towns such as Perth might earn them formal burgh status, galvanising the local economy. These burghs often developed on livestock trading routes (such as Roxburgh) or close to trading harbours (Berwick), although a few towns (Dunfermline, St Andrews) became burghs due to their cult, military or royal status. Royal burghs also acquired overseas trading rights.

Scotland's seventy or so burghs provided a degree of urban infrastructure, although – with the exception of Edinburgh – they were generally smaller than English towns and cities. Buildings in a burgh were often divided between human and animal occupancy, as in the countryside. Houses were typically built of timber, wattle, clay, dung, mud and thatch. In the kirktouns, houses would surround a central church (or kirk) of wood or slate and stone. Stone was only just beginning to be used for domestic dwellings and took some time to catch on, though by the sixteenth century tile and glass were common in the houses of prosperous burgesses. The well-to-do built homes overlooking the main street, often with a wooden gallery or balcony reached by an outside stair: merchants and traders had trading premises on the ground floor. Along a central street, the frontage of some houses was narrow due to competition for space. In time, many of the buildings fronting the main street became flats above shops.

Streets tended to run in parallel (St Andrews) or converge on a marketplace or church (Selkirk), with long strips of land or *lang riggs* behind each house. As time went on, brewhouses, granaries and kilns developed in these backlands, which in turn gave way to smaller streets leading off the main ones. Burgh trade was thus conducted both on the high street itself and from shops behind which were typically family businesses, with the family living above or behind the premises. This model lasted until at least the eighteenth century. Women were often heads of these households, and dominated certain trades such as brewing. Governance in the Scottish burghs could be surprisingly inclusive, too: not only were there female burgesses and legacies supporting female education, but in 1536 the town clerk of the small Aberdeenshire kirktoun of Inverurie seems to have been elected by both women and men.

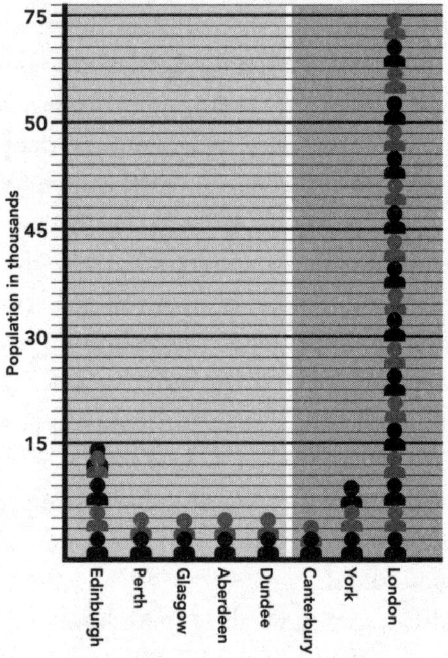

Burghs remained small and compact – as late as the seventeenth century Edinburgh town centre measured just 900 by 450 metres. Apart from the capital, only Aberdeen, Dundee, Glasgow and Perth could muster a population above 5,000 by 1550. The burgh became a place for entertainment, pageant and show – even riot, at times – with pipers, drummers or harpists a common feature, along with cockfighting and horseracing in later centuries. New fashions and technologies such as the 'horloge' were also in demand, though when Aberdeen acquired a town clock in 1450 there was no one able to maintain it.

Sexuality was regulated by the clerical authorities, who in the medieval era forbade marriage even between distant cousins sharing a common great-great-grandparent. In the cramped burghs, with their small, close-knit and relatively immobile populations, technical incest must have become hard to avoid. In the centuries after the Reformation, the sharing of close physical space by members of the opposite sex gave rise to a veritable industry of denunciation and repentance which could pack out the minutes of Kirk sessions.

Burghs exported wood, hides and salmon (the Aberdeen salmon kitemark was prized), later on cloth and wood, and later still coal. Salt was produced in Scotland from the eleventh century, and saltworks and salmon traps are evident in Moray in the north-east from the twelfth. The Hundred Years War (1337–1453) between England and France boosted demand for Scottish salt, interrupting the French supply chain. Scottish salt and coal production were protected – until the eighteenth century – by serious restrictions on the freedom of labourers in these industries. The herring and salmon trade was also lucrative. Though poor organisation hindered growth in customs revenues, fishing was an important source of royal revenue by the fifteenth century.

The Lübeck Letter

The Wars of Independence were highly disruptive to trade. As the famous Lübeck Letter of 11 October 1297 makes clear, Murray and Wallace were as keen to support commerce as they were to defend national rights.

> Andrew de Murray and William Wallace, leaders of the army of the kingdom of Scotland, and the community of the same kingdom, to their worthy, discreet and beloved friends the mayors and communes of Lübeck and Hamburg, greeting, and increase always of sincere friendship.
>
> It has been intimated to us by trustworthy merchants of the said kingdom of Scotland that you

> by your own goodwill are giving counsel, help and favour in all causes and business concerning us and our merchants, although our merits had not deserved this, and therefore all the more are we bound to you to give you thanks and a worthy recompense, to do which we are willing to be obliged to you; and we ask you that you will make it be proclaimed amongst your merchants that they can have secure access to all ports of the kingdom of Scotland with their merchandise since the kingdom of Scotland, thanks be to God, has by arms been recovered from the power of the English. Farewell.
>
> Given at Haddington in Scotland on the 11th day of October in the year of grace one thousand two hundred and ninety seven.
>
> We request moreover that you will see fit to forward the business of John Burnet and John Frere, our merchants, just as you wish us to forward the business of your merchants. Farewell.

Overland trade between burghs was improved by new ferries and bridges, though Scotland's rugged landscape meant transport was still easier by water. External trade was chiefly with the Baltic, the Low Countries and France – ahead of England and Ireland, a pattern that would only become more prominent in time. There were links with the late-Viking north, which stretched from Norway to Greenland and beyond, and these were complemented by northern European routes, including those plied by the Hanseatic League. The medieval Hansa commercial confederation eventually covered almost all the south Baltic coast and, like an early European Union, pursued common regulation among its partner cities.

By the later 1200s, Scottish merchants in Bruges were numerous enough to have a named quarter in the town. In other foreign cities too, trading enclaves captured the export business to Scotland. At Veere in the Netherlands, for example, the 'Conservator' of Scots privileges resided in the Scots House from 1541. But by this time adverse climate change, a devalued currency and a deteriorating trade position were beginning to undermine the home economy in Scotland. The upland climate north of Tay deteriorated from the fifteenth century. A nine-day sandstorm that buried the town of Forvie in Aberdeenshire in 1413 and the call for an intensified wolf hunt in 1428 both suggest greater volatility in the climate, which by the seventeenth century was causing habitation loss in the islands.

Even in a poorer climate, Scotland's slowly growing population could still feed itself, so the country tended to see lower levels of agrarian radicalism than elsewhere in Europe. Relative economic decline affected the whole country, but the south of Scotland, with its milder climate and less severe winters, began to dominate the economy as time went on. By the 1530s, customs accounts show the south as representing nearly 75 per cent of the Scottish total, with Edinburgh alone controlling half of the national export trade and other burghs in relative decline. In 1499, Edinburgh exported 73,000 skins; by the close of the following century, the total exceeded 400,000, while its share of Scottish cloth exports grew from 65 per cent in the 1470s to 80 per cent sixty years later.

Despite the concentration of urban wealth, more than half the population still lived north of the River Tay until as recently as the mid-eighteenth century. Many other Scots emigrated. By the 1600s there were some 30,000–50,000 Scots in Poland, the same number in Ireland and many in the Netherlands too. Emigration was to have a significant impact on Scots trading and educational patterns in the centuries to come. But it was evidence not only of the weaknesses of Scotland's rural economy but also the strengths of its highly developed education system and strong urban institutions.

The crest of the Hammermen of Glasgow today

Merchant and craft guilds grew up in the burghs. In Edinburgh there were more than a dozen incorporated trades, including Cordiners (1477), Goldsmiths (1525), Hammermen (1501) and Tailors (1446). In Glasgow there were the Hammermen, Tailors, Cordiners, Maltmen, Weavers, Bakers, Skinners, Wrights, Coopers, Fleshers, Masons, Gardeners, Barbers, and Dyers and Bonnetmakers. There were nine incorporated trades in Dundee, eight in Perth and seven in Stirling. By the sixteenth and seventeenth centuries these well-established crafts had their own systems of governance, the guilds, which allowed their collective strength to be more effectively counterpoised to that of the merchant classes. Glasgow, for example, developed both a Merchants' (established long before its official 1605 constitution) and a Trades House. The descendants of both still stand, although they were effectively displaced by the creation of Great Britain's first Chamber of Commerce in the city in 1783.

Wealth also flowed into the Church. Even in modest burghs there were sometimes abbeys and monasteries; and of course there were cathedrals in the cities, often boasting an impressive array of relics. In the fifteenth century, St Machar's in Aberdeen claimed to hold not only clothes of the Virgin Mary but also bones of St Peter, St Paul and St Margaret. As these cathedrals assumed a recognisably modern form between the twelfth and fourteenth centuries, places of learning grew up around them. In later centuries many of these schools – originally Catholic foundations – turned into the great burgh grammar schools such as the High School of Glasgow or Aberdeen Grammar School, which came into the hands of the local secular government following the Reformation.

By the 1400s priests who could not speak Gaelic were being appointed to parishes where many people did – the learned elite no longer acquired the language as a matter of course. Gaelic continued to decline in the urban centres where the burgh grammar schools and the universities were located. But the rise of the burghs also saw the rise of Scots, a language which, with a vocabulary of some 100,000 words (deriving from Anglo-Saxon, French, Latin, Norse and elsewhere) but limited grammatical distinction from English, was increasingly spoken and written throughout the country. Like Gaelic, Scots existed in different dialects across Scotland, but there was also something of a court standard. Although kings as late as James IV (r. 1488–1513) spoke Gaelic, Scots was becoming the language of public administration and of the nations' printed literature.

By the seventeenth century, Edinburgh – with more than 40,000 people – was the second-largest city on the island after London. Until the reign of James III (r. 1460–88) the court and parliament were mobile and there was no formal capital city. Royal progresses were times of great excitement, as during Queen Margaret's visit to Aberdeen in 1511, when she was welcomed with a pageant depicting King Robert and his successors, and maidens in green representing the fertility of the kingdom – and by implication its queen. Progresses were also cumbersome and expensive, however, with up to thirty-five carts needed for the queen's dresses alone. Both unity and awareness of cultural and social difference were on show at the court, with Scots ballads sung for the king. On occasion the monarch himself might even impersonate a local beggar or

Stirling Castle: royal architecture stressed the importance of the great hall

balladeer, as James V (r. 1513–42) is reputed to have done in his role as 'the Gudeman of Ballengeich' – Ballengeich being the area near his palace at Stirling. The architecture of the royal palaces themselves, at Stirling, Edinburgh, Linlithgow and Falkland, continued in many cases to lay stress on the communal space of the great hall, rather than the more exclusive, specialist architecture of contemporary palaces of the European Renaissance on show elsewhere.

Balance of Power and the Auld Alliance

For all its cultural differences, Scotland retained close ties to the Continent. These owed as much to politics as to trade. During the Hundred Years War, Scotland had invaded England as part of its obligation to France under the Auld Alliance, only for David II to be captured by the English at the Battle of Neville's Cross just outside Durham in 1346. He was eventually released after the English victory at Poitiers ten years later.

Later Scottish victories at Lochmaben (1384) and Otterburn (1388) in the reign of Robert II (r. 1371–90) kept the balance of power on the English border. They were accompanied by an intensifying Scottish patriotism. In 1385, parliament ordered the Saltire, the white cross of St Andrew, to be carried on the front and back of Scottish soldiers – 150 years before England's King Henry VIII (r. 1509–47) followed suit with the St George's Cross. Towards the end of the Hundred Years War, Scottish troops were able to significantly reinforce France: around 15,000 were in the service of the French Crown in the 1419–24 period. At Baugé in March 1421, the forces of John Stewart, Earl of Buchan triumphed over the Duke of Clarence's English army. Buchan subsequently became Constable of France before being defeated and killed in 1424 at Verneuil, where the victorious English army showed no quarter to the Scots.

The Auld Alliance between Scotland and France was perhaps at its strongest in the fifteenth and sixteenth centuries. Tradition has it that the Scots air 'Hey tutti taiti' (now known as 'Scots Wha Hae' and in France as '*Marche des soldats de Robert Bruce*' or '*Hymne de Sainte Jeanne d'Arc*') was played as French and Scottish troops relieved the siege of Orléans at the turning point of the Hundred Years War in 1429. Set for pipes, drums and brass, it is still performed to this day at solemn moments in France. The 'Street of the Sword of Scotland' in Orléans commemorates the liberation of the city, and several Scottish commanders have their own memorials: John Stewart of Darnley was buried in its cathedral. On her entry into Orléans, Joan of Arc was welcomed by its bishop, John Kirkmichael, a Scotsman from Fife.

The Scottish connection with France went far beyond the purely military. In the fifteenth century some 15,000 Scots were living in France. In later centuries it remained easy to settle there: Scots received similar treatment to French subjects in terms of inheritance, and were readily naturalised. It was only at the dawn of the twentieth century that these rights were finally withdrawn. Scots were also heavily involved in business and the professions – particularly in French higher education, where a dozen rectors of the University of Paris alone were Scots. Later, every one of France's Huguenot colleges was to have a Scottish principal at some time or another. French architecture remained influential in Scotland, not only on the Netherbow port in Edinburgh (demolished in 1764), but also on Holyroodhouse, which echoed the Loire châteaux. The vast tenement blocks of Edinburgh were built with those of Paris and other French cities firmly in mind.

Holyrood Palace – gateway, 1746. Sketch by Thomas Sandby. The great château-like bastions are visible in the background.

> It is statute and ordanit throw all the realme that all barronis and frehaldaris that ar of substance put their eldest sonnis and airis to the sculis fra thai be aucht or nyne yeiris of age and till remane at the grammer sculis quhill that be competentlie foundit and have perfite latyne and thereftir to remane thre yeiris at the sculis of art and jure sua that thai may have knawledge and understanding of the lawis.
>
> 1496 Education Act

At home, the traditional Scottish emphasis on education was already clear. By the time of the 1496 Education Act in the reign of James IV, there were already a large number of burgh schools in place. These were often linked to the expanded religious foundations of the era of David I. Schools were founded at Glasgow (1124), Edinburgh (1128), Stirling (1129), Lanark (1183), Ayr (1233) and Dundee (1239), while universities were founded at St Andrews (1411), Glasgow (1451) and King's College Aberdeen (1495). These institutions already boasted considerable scholars, such as Laurence of Lindores (St Andrews), John Mair, formerly professor at Paris (St Andrews) and Hector Boece (Aberdeen).

Much of the energy of Scottish culture was directed towards forging a distinct national identity. Poets and chroniclers such as John Barbour (*c.* 1320–95), Archdeacon of Aberdeen, his contemporary and fellow Aberdonian priest John of Fordoun (d. 1384) and the Abbot of Inchcolm, Walter Bower (*c.* 1385–1449), presented a vision of the historic Scottish nation coloured by its recent struggles for freedom, giving of course – they were all priests – due weight to the country's powerful Church. As Bower wrote at the end of his magisterial *Scotichronicon*, a chronicle of the nation's history, '*Non Scotus est Christe cui libet non placet iste*' ('Christ! he is no Scot who does not like this book'). In the following century, Boece injected Tacitus' *Agricola* into the heart of his own *Scotorum Historia,* converting the Roman writer's Republican rhetoric into a vision of Scotland's struggle against England. With shades of the Declaration of Arbroath, this was to be a key feature of the Scoto-Romanism that lasted well into the eighteenth century, shaping the identity of the Scottish elite in Roman terms. Even today, senior judges in Scotland are Senators of the College of Justice, with a cultural heritage that identifies them with the Roman magistracy. From the foundation of the College in 1532, the practice of the law in Scotland was much more closely linked to the nobility than was the case in England. It was more a ruling magistracy than a middle-class profession.

'Our Awyn Langage'

The creation of a Scots literature likewise belongs to the era of Barbour and his successors. Robert Henryson (*c.* 1430–*c.* 1498), sometime staff member of the University of Glasgow and later master of the burgh grammar school in Dunfermline, presented the classical themes of Homer, Aesop and Chaucer in Scots vernacular, while the powerful lyrics of the bawdy priest William Dunbar (*c.* 1459/60–1517/30) still carry a contemporary beat and relevance. *Wallace* by the epic polemicist Blin Hary (*c.* 1440–92) was the most nationalist work of the day. Hary was a poetic advocate of resistance to England: his couplet 'A false usurper sinks in every foe / And liberty returns with every blow' was later adapted by Burns, who described it as 'worthy of Homer'.

If Hary represents the passionately national among the poets of the Stewart era, then Gavin Douglas (1474/6–1522), who died in England while attending the court of Henry VIII, represents the cosmopolitan side of Scottish culture, with his pioneering translation of Virgil's *Aeneid* (1513). Yet even Douglas promises in his translation to use *'na sudron, bot our awyn langage'* ('no Southron [English] but our own language'). All over Europe the learned classes were replacing Latin with their own local vernaculars, but Scotland was in the van. The language used was called 'Scottis' or Scots. On some occasions, this could sound very much like a variety of English. On others, its formations – particularly in high-flown register – were unlike anything English had to offer, as in Dunbar's poem to the Blessed Virgin Mary:

> Hale, sterne superne, hale, in eterne
>   In Godis sicht to schyne,
> Lucerne in derne for to discerne,
>   Be glory and grace devyne,
> Hodiern, modern, sempitern,
>   Angelicall regyne ...
>
> [Hail, eternal star of Heaven
> Shining in the sight of God,

Discerning light in darkness,
By God's glory and grace,
Today, of our times and eternally,
Queen of the angels ...]

Royal and aristocratic patronage prevailed in Scotland, as in other European states. The music of Robert Carver, Canon of Scone Abbey (*c.* 1485/6–1568/70) – the motet *O bone Jesu* for nineteen voices, for example – reflects the substantial musical resources available to Scotland's religious houses, and *Pater Creator Omnium* remains among the most powerful sung masses of the era. James III, IV and V were all generous patrons of the arts from the mid-fifteenth to mid-sixteenth centuries, with Sir David Lindsay's classic social satire on the nature of good governance, *Ane Plesant Satyre of the Thrie Estaitis* (1540), being performed for James V (r. 1513–42) at Linlithgow Palace in 1540.

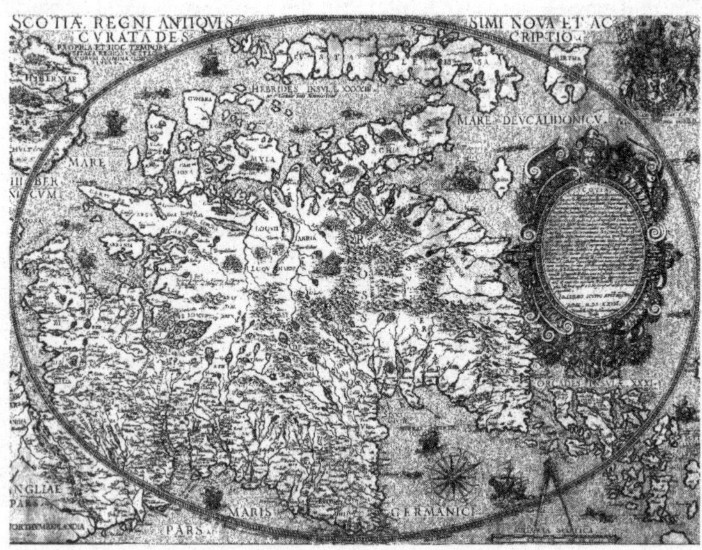

John Leslie's map of Scotland, 1578

It is during this period that the 'Highlands' and the 'Lowlands' emerged as distinct places of the imagination. In time the idea of a social, cultural and even political divide running through Scotland would become the subject of everything from high romantic literature to low propaganda. Yet if one examines early maps, it is the counties or their associated earldoms that are most clearly marked, rather than any internal ethno-cultural division allegedly cutting across them.

The parts of Scotland in which Gaelic was spoken in 1400 extended well beyond any area that could be termed the 'Highlands', and included Angus, some of Ayrshire, Stirlingshire and other mostly lowland areas. While there are scattered mentions of 'Highlanders' in fourteenth- and fifteenth-century Scots writing, the references are often formulaic and should be taken with a pinch of salt. To give only one example, William Dunbar's supposed 'anti-Highland' sentiments are actually part of a 'flyting' poem designed for the exchange of insults – and besides, the target of his jibes is an Ayrshireman.

The Crown itself adopted tartan at this time as a means of representing the ancestral Scottishness of the dynasty. Both James V and Mary Queen of Scots (r. 1542–67) chose to wear 'Highland' attire, rather than dressing to emphasise the separation of their urban court from the Gaelic world. Tartan was reported as being worn by many women in Edinburgh well into the eighteenth century.

The figure of Alexander Stewart (1343–1405) illustrates the problem with ascribing crude 'Highland' or 'Lowland' labels in this period. Alexander's misbehaviour as Lord of Badenoch – he spectacularly abused his position as justiciar in the north and burnt Elgin Cathedral in 1390 – is sometimes seen as a source of anti-Highland feeling and earned him the sobriquet 'Wolf of Badenoch'. Yet as the son of King Robert II, the Wolf issued from the 'Lowland' House of Stewart. To complicate matters further, he was married to the Countess of Ross and was thus brother-in-law to John, Lord of the Isles – both of them on any account Highlanders. The identity of the Wolf of Badenoch cannot therefore be easily pinned down, nor his exploits fitted to a narrative of intercultural conflict within Scotland. The battle of Harlaw (1411), fought by two of his kinsmen over the succession to the Earldom of Ross and often mythologised as a classic 'Highland vs Lowland' encounter, was in fact a dynastic struggle over bragging rights in the north.

The Wolf's Lair: Lochindorb Castle in Badenoch, stronghold of Alexander Stewart

Undoubtedly the bonds of loyalty differed between Scottish magnates and their followers in different parts of the country, and the balance between kinship, association and feudal practice varied from place to place. The Lord of the Isles was difficult for the Crown to control because he was remote, not because he was culturally 'Gaelic' – Robert the Bruce's homeland of Carrick in Ayrshire was Gaelic, too. Ultimately the remote lords were also part of a single Scottish polity under 'the Lyon' – the King of Scots and his royal standard.

Internal conflicts typically arose from disputes over territory, not least those caused by the contradictory and confusing land grants over MacDonald holdings in the western Lordship of the Isles. Such squabbles were curtailed by the Crown, which relied on the great magnates Argyll and Huntly to act as its viceroys in the west and north respectively. The Crown itself gradually centralised power, though not as effectively as Henry VII (r. 1485–1509) was able to achieve in England. James II (r. 1437–60) annexed many Douglas lordships to the Crown, despite the risks: his father James I was murdered by dissident nobles. Remote magnates such as the Lords of the Isles often tried to play off Scotland and England to preserve their power, as their Galloway predecessors had done three centuries earlier, but with less success over time.

The monarchs of Scotland themselves became more integrated into the royal families of Europe, as the King of Scots sought equal status with his continental contemporaries. Earlier kings had often married the daughters of earls and chiefs, or at best English kings, but James III married the daughter of the King of Denmark; James IV, the daughter of Henry VII; and James V, the daughters of the King of France and the Duc de Guise. Only Mary of Scotland's marriages after 1560 reversed this pattern – and thereby demonstrated her weakness and vulnerability. As a Catholic queen caught in a Protestant religious crisis, she was always going to find the exertion of power challenging.

Throughout this period, Gaelic Scotland retained a different language and distinctive elements of the culture from which it came. It's worth remembering, however, that most of Scotland had been Gaelic-speaking at some point and so shared this cultural touchstone. In the run-up to the Battle of Flodden (1513), poets called in Gaelic for 'no gentle warfare' against the 'Saxon' English: 'burn their bad coarse wives, burn their uncouth offspring' was one particularly unpleasant poetic exhortation, addressed to Archibald, the Earl of Argyll, who was nevertheless killed on the battlefield.

Fallen Flower of Scotland

The defeat at Flodden in 1513 was the largest that had ever been inflicted on a Scottish army: some 40,000 men gathered, of whom more than 30,000 fought in the battle. It was the first time in five centuries that a Scots king had been killed in combat with a foreign power. Worse, the slaughter inflicted on the army was tragically unnecessary: a smaller diversionary attack could have achieved at far less cost their aim of honouring the Auld Alliance by supporting the French king, Louis XII, against Henry VIII of England.

Bad strategic judgement was compounded by foolhardy tactics. The English commanders stood at the rear, King James IV led from the front. With him fell the Archbishop of St Andrews, the Bishop of the Isles, the Lord High Treasurer of Scotland and the Earls of Argyll, Bothwell, Caithness, Cassilis, Crawford, Erroll, Lennox, Montrose, Morton and Rothes as well as many other noblemen, including the Chiefs of the Name of Macfarlane and Maclean. It was a massacre of the ruling class and Scotland had never experienced a defeat like it. Contemporaries thought it a foolish battle, fought foolishly.

Many parts of Scotland suffered dreadfully from the loss of young men. The famous song 'The Flowers of the Forest' refers to the eighty men raised from Selkirk Forest to be the king's Archers' Guard (the ancestor of today's Royal Company of Archers), of whom only one returned alive.

Henry VIII: Aggressive Reform

James IV's death at Flodden left his wife Margaret Tudor (Henry VIII's sister) Queen Dowager of Scotland. Initially a General Council of the Realm ruled in her name and that of her son, the infant James V (r. 1513–42), before John Stewart, Duke of Albany, returned from France to rule as regent from 1515.

Even before Henry VIII's Reformation in the 1530s, the Scottish Crown had been valuable to the papacy and the Catholic powers. Now, with Henry facing dissent from the North of England, it was feared that an adult James V would invade with European back-up. The offer of the kingship of Ireland to James by rebels there can only have reinforced Henry's desire to integrate Ireland as a kingdom into his English 'empire' in 1541.

Determined to end the threat from a Catholic enemy in the north, Henry despatched English troops into Scotland in 1542. They were defeated at Haddon Rig near Kelso by an army under the Earl of Huntly in August, but this significant Scottish victory was overshadowed by the battle to come. When Henry demanded that James – his nephew – convert to the Reformed cause, the King of Scots refused and ordered his troops to march south. The invasion ended in total fiasco at Solway Moss in November, where the Scots were trapped between river and bogland. Many nobles surrendered.

James V died two weeks later, by tradition after hearing that his wife, Marie de Guise, had borne a daughter and not a son. Whatever the reason, the Scottish king can have had little hope that an infant girl could offer any resistance to the Tudor tyrant, whose war chest was swollen with the revenues of England's plundered monasteries. Ten of the twenty-three Scots lords captured at Solway Moss agreed to serve King Henry's interest. The English king demanded the surrender of the major Scottish castles, the end of the alliance with France and the removal of the Princess Marie/Mary to England, where she could be raised as the prospective wife of his son.

On 9 September, still less than a year old, Mary was crowned Queen of Scots. The next spring, the Earl of Hertford invaded and the infant queen was taken to Dunkeld. Hertford burnt Edinburgh and took control of most of southern Scotland. A

The invasion of Edinburgh, 1544: Holyrood Palace; English troops entering the Canongate

respite was gained by the victory of Scottish forces at Ancrum near Jedburgh in early 1545, but the crisis was far from over. Henry encouraged a Protestant insurgency in Scotland, leading to the murder of the patriot Cardinal Beaton in 1546 by John Knox and others, who seized St Andrews Castle in the process.

A Blast of the Trumpet: John Knox (c. *1514–72)*

Portrait of John Knox, 1572

John Knox was long seen as one of the pivotal figures of Scottish history, though he has become less popular as a historical protagonist in the past hundred years. He came to prominence with his role in the murder of Cardinal Beaton on 29 May 1546, after his fellow Reformer – and suspected English spy – George Wishart was executed with the cardinal's consent. Knox was taken prisoner by the French in 1547, sentenced to the galleys, and released in 1549, whereupon he joined the Church of England and eventually became chaplain to King Edward VI (r. 1547–53), marrying an Englishwoman, Margery Bowes.

On the accession in England of Mary Tudor (r. 1553–8), who pledged to restore Catholicism, Knox left for exile to Geneva, where he met and was deeply influenced by John Calvin. Knox's *The First Blast of the Trumpet Against the Monstrous Regiment of Women* (1558) was written against Mary of England, Marie de Guise in Scotland and her daughter Mary Queen of Scots. The new Protestant English monarch Elizabeth was not a target – Knox's misogyny was sectarian – but she nonetheless declined to offer him a passport to return to Scotland in 1559.

When he eventually came back home, he at once became a useful front man for the pro-Reform nobles, known as the Lords of the Congregation, who opposed Marie de Guise. When the Franco-Scottish Crown sent French troops against the Protestant rebels, Knox appealed to England. As a consequence of the Treaty of Berwick in February 1560, English troops arrived in Scotland to support the Protestant interest in March.

Three months later, Marie de Guise died and the Reformation was well on the way to triumphing in Scotland. So began the first stirrings of a major political realignment in which the alliance between Church and Crown on which the Scottish nation had been built was irreversibly damaged. Knox helped write the foundational documents for the new Reformed Church in Scotland, such as the Confession of Faith, and served as religious leader of the reformed community after the return of Mary Queen of Scots to

Edinburgh in 1561. Despite her policy of tolerance, Knox pursued the Catholic queen with deep-seated hostility, calling openly for her death from 1566.

In his *History of the Reformation in Scotland*, written in five volumes in the same year, Knox lingered on his own career achievements, doing much to burnish his posthumous reputation. Although he supported the Reformed tradition of Church governance known as Presbyterianism and is remembered as one of its founders, he was not opposed to bishops (provided they were Protestant), eschewing the hysterical opposition to them which became a characteristic of many of his successors. His influence on the practice and ethos of Scottish Presbyterianism was very great, as was his legacy to English Puritanism.

On 10 September 1547, the Duke of Somerset, Protector of England during Edward VI's (r. 1547–53) minority, defeated Arran's army at Pinkie Cleugh near Edinburgh. The Scottish Privy Council appealed for help to France and the next year the queen was promised in marriage to the Dauphin in return for French troops. England once again invaded and by August 1548 Mary was in France. Despite Somerset's appeal for a united Protestant 'Empire of Great Britain' – one of the first uses of the term – and his more practical goal of creating an English buffer zone in Scotland, French troops were now present in force and sent England and its Scottish supporters into retreat, driving them back to a few strongholds. Meanwhile Henri II (r. 1547–59) attacked the remaining English possessions in France.

After spending a colossal fortune on trying to forge dynastic and religious union with Scotland through warfare, England's worst nightmares about the Auld Alliance were coming true. King Edward made peace. Somerset was the scapegoat, executed in January 1552 as a coda to his ruinous policy. In 1558, Mary married the Dauphin and in 1559 she became Queen of France. The regnal union of Scotland and France was celebrated in medals and coinage. Scottish coins carried the legend, *'Iam non sunt duo sed una caro'* ('They are no longer two but one flesh'), referring both to the marriage and to the kingdoms, for the royal couple were celebrated as 'Francis and Mary, King and Queen of Scotland'. History seemed about to change course.

This twelvepence groat, minted in 1559, represents the union of Scotland and France after the marriage of Mary and Francis (note the crowned dolphin and thistle on either side of the monogram).

Then on 11 June 1560, Mary's mother, the queen dowager Marie, died in Scotland. Six months later, Mary's husband died in France. Both were lottery wins for the young Queen Elizabeth in England, who herself had only recently come to the throne. The Protestant cause was generally reinforced, and France's interest in Scotland and commitment to it waned overnight. The Queen of France was now a childless dowager and Scotland's own queen dowager, eldest daughter of one of the most powerful houses in France, was dead. So convenient was this for Elizabeth that it has been suggested that Marie de Guise

Mary Queen of Scots. Portrait after François Clouet. Charles I kept this version in the Cabinet Room at Whitehall Palace.

was poisoned by the English queen's agents, but dropsy is more likely to have been the culprit. As for Mary, she had lost her husband and her mother and now returned to a country much changed from the patriot Catholic kingdom of her infancy, with Protestant lords in the ascendant.

Sweeping Reform

The Reformation in Scotland felt like a much more significant break with the past than in England, where efforts were made to weave a fiction of continuity even as royal policy swung to and fro. Henry's regime, with its lingering allegiances to Catholic practice, gave way a more aggressively evangelical Protestantism under Edward VI, then the restoration of Catholicism under Mary, followed by the Anglican settlement under Elizabeth (r. 1558–1603). Despite the ruination of the monasteries, many secular clergy kept their churches and their livings during these decades, believing today what might be forsworn tomorrow. Even the Archbishop of Canterbury, Thomas Cranmer, had to hide his wife from the king when Henry's Parliament decided in favour of unmarried clergy in 1539.

In Scotland the religious change was deeper and its foreign policy consequences were greater. Although the Reformation in Scotland resembled more the reforms of Continental Europe than those in England, it kickstarted a process that in the end made Scotland less European by drawing the country gradually out of France's orbit. It did help to deepen links with the Protestant Netherlands, but only France had the might to effectively defend Scotland through force of arms.

This change did not happen all at once. Scots remained prominent in France and kept rights of settlement, serving in the French military into the second half of the eighteenth century. Some features of the Auld Alliance survived. Yet the Reformation marked the beginning of a lasting split between the two countries. As Scotland drew closer to the Netherlands and then – through royal marriage – to the kingdom of Denmark-Norway, it found itself increasingly at loggerheads with the Catholic powers of Europe. A vast number of Scots – perhaps 100,000 in all – joined the Thirty Years War (1618–48) on the Protestant side, before continuing the fight at home against King Charles I (r. 1625–49) and his religious settlement. In effect, the Reformation frayed Scotland's ties with its only allied superpower in favour of much smaller European countries that could not protect it, and underpinned almost two centuries of intermittent civil, national and international conflict.

The Church in Scotland was divided between Episcopalian and Presbyterian interests. People differed little in terms of their fundamental beliefs, but the issue of bishops and Church governance generated much tribalistic conflict. Perennial religious strife, combined with liberal helpings of plague and famine and the constant drain of emigration, meant that the population in 1755 was hardly any bigger at 1.1 million than it had been in the 1640s – or, for that matter, the fourteenth century.

Scotland's religious houses had been a growing burden at a time of economic decline, and the chance to lighten that load made the Reformation more popular. With English help, the pro-reform nobles known as the Lords of the Congregation gained the upper hand, pushing through legislation in

Parliament to reject papal supremacy and adopt Protestantism. John Knox then led this in a Presbyterian direction – that is, towards a Scottish Kirk wihout bishops. Churches and cathedrals were attacked and asset-stripped, though not on a systematic basis as in England.

Some parts of the country were resistant to Presbyterianism, notably the country north of the Tay, where contact with Scandinavia and the Baltic and German states had made Lutheranism more popular than Calvinism. (Very broadly speaking, the difference was similar to that between the Church of England and the Puritans, with hardline Calvinists seeing Lutheran beliefs as a watered-down Catholicism.) Other parts of Scotland kept their allegiance to Rome, notably Banffshire and the north-western seaboard and some of the more remote islands. In 1600, some English sources suggested that a third of the Scottish nobility still had Catholic sympathies.

From the beginning, Reformation ideas were bound up with elements of pro-English feeling. When Mary returned to Scotland in 1561, she found herself in a weak position, isolated from her most powerful allies amidst a climate of sectarian misogyny. In English minds she became a figure the poet Edmund Spenser (1552–99) called 'Duessa', the double-dealing Catholic whore who endangered the rule of Protestant Truth – in other words, the 'Faerie Queen' Elizabeth. Deposed in Scotland in favour of her son, the infant James VI, Mary fled to England in 1568.

It was an unwise move. After almost twenty years' imprisonment, she was beheaded on 8 February 1587. Aware of the constitutional implications of executing an anointed sovereign and dowager queen of France, Elizabeth had initially sought Mary's murder. In the end, however, she plumped for what was at least the appearance of judicial process.

Mary, like her mother, was fairly moderate in her Catholic views, but the atmosphere in Europe at the time of her death was uncompromising and toxic. The killing of a Catholic queen, combined with an English raid on Cádiz in 1587 and Elizabeth's support for Dutch resistance to Spain, gave cause for the attempted invasion of England by the Spanish Armada in 1588. Positions on both sides were extreme: Pope Sixtus V treated the Armada to all intents and purposes as a crusade, while Elizabeth's government tortured Catholic clergy to death. In Scotland and England alike, these were perilous times for people of religious conscience.

James VI of Scotland, James I of England

Mary's son, the young King James VI of Scotland, survived a dangerous childhood beset by plots. In 1585, in early adulthood, he helped secure a defensive alliance with England, a move that surely smoothed the way for his accession to the English throne on Elizabeth's death in 1603. Scotland remained an independent state, but James I of England (as he would be known south of the border) moved to London.

England, Scotland and Ireland now formed a composite monarchy: three discrete countries under a single crown. This kind of arrangement was widespread in Europe, but was not well suited to the British Isles, where England (and more particularly London) was determined to remain the dominant force. James' attempts to forge a closer Union between England and Scotland were opposed by his parliament at Westminster, and while an early version of what became the Union flag appeared, it was only permitted to be flown together with the flag of England or Scotland. In 1634, it became reserved for Crown service only.

Edinburgh Castle by John Slezer, 1693, showing the pre-1707 Union flag

Scotland felt the pull of the new centre of gravity in London. The Scottish Privy Council grew anxious that it should be consulted on treaties and not have its consent assumed by the king, and the Scottish Convention of Royal Burghs appointed a lobbyist in the English capital in 1613. Within Scotland, the Bond and Statutes of Iona (1609) curbed the autonomy of Gaelic-speaking chiefs and their freedom to practice the Catholic faith. Emigration from the isles continued, spurred by the opportunity under a new composite monarchy for Scots to settle in northern Ireland in large numbers.

Although Scotland remained independent, hopes of forging a separate foreign policy were jeopardised by the fact that diplomats were appointed by the Crown and not Parliament – although James did appoint some Scots, he usually appointed them to represent *all* his realms. The king returned to Scotland only once in all the years after his accession to the English throne, in 1617. By the 1620s, foreign ambassadors were leaving the country.

Conflict became the hallmark of the seventeenth century,

which saw more Scots in arms than ever before. Between 1618 and 1694, Scotland was far more often than not involved in either civil conflict or overseas warfare, further stressing an already lacklustre economy. The fierce doctrinal divisions of the age fired acts of religious terrorism and violence, in bitter contrast to the unified patriot church that had once defended Scotland. Ninian Winyet (1519–92), distinguished Scottish exile and Abbot of Ratisbon, complained of the growth of the English language at the expense of Scots in Protestant discourse in Scotland; by 1617, interpreters were no longer thought to be necessary in London.

Scotland's conflicts were intimately linked to the wider Thirty Years War (1618–48). The wars of Reformation and counter-Reformation that began in the sixteenth century grew into in a continent-wide struggle between, on the one side, the Habsburgs of Spain and the Holy Roman Empire, and on the other, Bohemia, France and a range of northern European Protestant states including the Dutch Republic. Scotland entered the conflict on the side of the Protestant monarch of Bohemia, Frederick V, who was married to James VI's daughter Elizabeth. The Scots elite raised an army to fight for her, and before the war was over more than 50,000 and perhaps as many as 100,000 Scots had served this cause (with a small but not insignificant number joining the Catholic powers on the other side).

By 1637 the Protestant wars abroad were coming home, as 300 veteran officers from the Swedish service returned to Scotland and leading players in the Scottish state prepared to open a northern front. In 1637, Archbishop Laud's Scottish Prayer Book was introduced to public worship, drawing the Protestants of Scotland into much closer conformity with the Church of England than many found comfortable. A National

Covenant was drafted in response, opposing any such religious innovations in Scotland. It was publicly adopted at Greyfriars Kirkyard in Edinburgh on 28 February 1638.

A Sovereign Right of Resistance

The wording of the Covenant concludes with a bond which commits its co-signatories to defend the nation's religion in its current form. Technically it upheld the authority of the Crown and was sufficiently ambiguous to allow for some Episcopalians (supporters of government by bishops, loosely aligned with the Church of England) to support it. Nonetheless, the Covenant became the founding document of militant Presbyterianism, upheld by the veterans of the Continental front in the Thirty Years War. It was an attempt both to resist English demands for ecclesial conformity, and to express a notion of popular sovereignty. The Covenant's supporters believed that it conferred a right of resistance by force of arms if necessary – and that is exactly what happened.

The Army of the Covenant was commanded by Field Marshal Alexander Leslie, newly returned from the Continental wars. A large number of his men, too, were veterans of the Swedish service, and their military expertise helped secure victory over Charles I's forces in the two brief 'Bishops' Wars' of 1639–40. When Charles threatened to ally with Spain in return for troops to defeat the Covenanters, they responded in kind, with the threat of a Scoto-Dutch alliance.

A Catholic rising in Ireland in 1641 intensified the collapse of Charles' government, though the Covenanters – eager to defend their fellow Protestants in northern Ireland – now offered the king troops (albeit under Scottish command) against the still greater common threat of Catholicism. General Robert Monro, a former Swedish colonel, landed in Ireland in

April 1642 with a Scottish Covenanting army whose main goal was to protect the Ulster Scots, while Eoghan Ruadh Ó Néill, commander of one of the seven Irish regiments in the Spanish service, landed in Donegal to take command of the forces of the Catholic Confederation, which had requested money and arms from Spain.

In England, war broke out between Crown and Parliament, who feared both Irish Catholic support for the king and the growing power of the Anglican Church. What is often called 'the English Civil War' was in reality a branch of the great convulsion that gripped the whole of Europe in 1618–48.

Solemn League

In 1643, the Scots Covenanters agreed a Solemn League and Covenant with English Parliamentarians. The reward for Parliament was the military support of the most formidable fighting force in the islands in their struggle against the Crown. They took this readily, without seriously intending to follow the Scots' religious terms. For their part, the Covenanters resolved to impose Presbyterian Church government on the whole of the British Isles. It was a mirror image of the king's strategy during the 1630s to impose Anglicanism in Scotland: the defensive patriotism of the original Covenant had grown into an imperial claim to extend Scottish Presbyterianism throughout the British kingdoms. The price of the Solemn League for Scotland was a form of closer religious and political association with England – though one still far short of the eventual political Union of 1707.

The League was of immediate and immense benefit to the English parliamentary war effort. When the Allied Army of Both Kingdoms won a critical victory at Marston Moor against the king in 1644, almost 60 per cent of its forces were comprised of Scottish troops. Yet there were dissenters. The Solemn League alienated some of the supporters of the older National Covenant, and as time went on it excluded others. The Marquis of Montrose opposed the hegemonic pretensions of the Solemn League and led a mixed Scottish and Irish army on behalf of the king. Montrose's men won many victories in Scotland – often skilfully exploiting the strategic advantages of mountain and flood – before at last being defeated at Philiphaugh on their march south in 1645.

The League's commanders made a number of poor decisions. After Charles I was executed, the Scottish Parliament chose to back Charles II (r. 1649–85) to succeed his father as king – on condition he kept the Covenant (he had as little intention of doing so as did the English Parliament). This led to defeats of Scottish forces at Dunbar (1650) and Worcester (1651) by Oliver Cromwell's Parliamentarian forces. Later, Cromwell – from 1653 Lord Protector and effective dictator – was able to incorporate Scotland as well as Ireland into a single Commonwealth. Cromwell temporarily ended the composite monarchy and its separate administration of three kingdoms, though the Commonwealth retained the title of 'England, Scotland and Ireland' rather than 'Britain'. Many Scots who had fought against Cromwell were shipped out to North America and the Caribbean, a practice that would endure deep into the eighteenth century: 900 to Virginia and 150 to New England in 1651, 6,000 to the American colonies and the Caribbean the following year.

Charles II was restored to the throne of all three kingdoms in 1660, and with him came the return of the composite monarchy. In Scotland, the restoration of the episcopal church with the Archbishop of St Andrews as its primate seemed to signal final defeat for the Covenanters. Yet religious violence lingered, and

The 'downsitting' (i.e. beginning) of the Scottish Parliament, 1685, from the *Atlas historique* of Nicolas de Gueudeville

a minority of the defeated Covenanters in central and western Scotland continued to foment trouble, including armed insurrections in 1666 and 1679. It was only after open rebellion broke out that royal policy turned decisively to stamping out this irreconcilable minority. Continued unrest – including the brutal murder of the archbishop in 1679 – deepened the cycle of repression. Though its victims were referred to as 'the Covenanters', in reality only a small fraction remained of those who bore that title in the 1640s and became mythologised as martyrs after the 1680s.

The Church of Scotland

The Church of Scotland – the Kirk – was far more than a Presbyterian version of the Church of England. It wielded considerable social authority into the nineteenth century, and was a participant in many of the intellectual and ideological debates within Scottish society from the Enlightenment onwards. Kirk moderates developed a notion of Christianity with a social mission that was far removed from the anti-clerical stereotypes of Enlightenment thinkers in much of Continental Europe.

Landlordism was a crucial topic of debate. The right of secular landlords to nominate clergy to their livings was far more controversial in Presbyterian Scotland than in Anglican England. The dispute over patronage would definitively split the Kirk in 1843 after multiple earlier secessions. The row began in earnest in 1712 when the British Patronage Act gave landowners a legal right to appoint clergy to vacant church offices. When the General Assembly of the Church of Scotland lost its capacity to veto such appointments, dissenters swelled the ranks of the extreme Covenanters who had remained outside the established Kirk.

Opposition to the British constitution remained strong – most of all to oaths of loyalty or conformity imposed by the state on members of the Kirk. The burgess oath of 1747, taken in Edinburgh, Glasgow and Perth, was seen as a particularly noxious example of secular influence over the Kirk on a par with landlordism. Churchgoers split between those who would and those who would not take the oaths: the 'Burgher' and 'Anti-Burgher' congregations. By the 1770s there were nearly 200 dissenting Presbyterian groups in Scotland. Arguments over doctrine rumbled on over the decades, causing still more fragmentation. The largest secession of all took place in the Disruption of 1843, when the 'Free Kirk' split from the Kirk over the long-festering sore of patronage (finally abolished in 1874).

Congregations of all persuasions have dwindled in the

modern era. In the 2020s, the Kirk had just over 250,000 members and the Free Kirk 8,000, with smaller groups including the Continuing Free Kirk (formed in 2000), the Free Presbyterians, the Reformed Presbyterians and the Associated (ex-Free) Presbyterians. The doctrinal roads of Scottish Presbyterianism are thorny and fissiparous, and for most Scots today its ways are remote. Nonetheless, the Reformation created by their ancestors transformed Scotland and its relations with the rest of the world. Presbyterian Scotland may be a shadow of its former self, but from Ulster Unionism to Hebridean Calvinism, from social conformity to egalitarianism, its legacy lives on.

'Glorious' Revolution and Aftermath

After the deposition in 1689 of Charles II's successor James (VII of Scotland and II of England), the Episcopalian bishops proved reluctant to support the new King William III (r. 1689–1702). Under William, Presbyterianism was instituted as the 'Kirk by law established' in Scotland in 1690. Though it excluded a small number of Covenanters, the Kirk of Scotland praised the integrity of those who had died under the governments of Charles and James, while itself maintaining loyalty to William and his Queen Mary. As before, neither sovereign had any intention or interest in signing or honouring the Covenant. Instead, this revised bargain – Presbyterian privilege in return for collaboration with (after 1707) a non-Presbyterian state – continued to cause fissures in the Kirk of Scotland well into the nineteenth century and beyond.

James VII of Scotland had been deposed in a political storm that some called the 'Glorious Revolution' – implying, inaccurately, that it was a bloodless coup. It had begun with the birth on 10 June 1688 of an heir to the throne who would be brought up Catholic, spurring a number of Whig lords to contact James's nephew and son-in-law William of Orange and request his intervention to prevent a Catholic line of succession from developing in an Anglican state. The Prince of Orange landed at Torbay on 5 November with a multinational army of about 15,000 men. James's indecision and inability to respond led to desertions and eventually the king's own flight. The English Parliament then conferred the English crown jointly on William and his wife, James's daughter Mary (1658–94).

In Scotland as in Ireland, war swiftly followed between the new king's supporters and those nobles who refused to take the oath. The atrocities of that war, which lasted for six years, include the Massacre of Glencoe in 1692, when Scottish troops billeted in the houses of the MacDonalds of Glencoe murdered their hosts on the grounds that they had not sworn allegiance to William. The Scottish Parliament's inquiry into that massacre as a 'murder under trust' – because it included the abuse of hospitality – spared the king who authorised it. It was nonetheless embarrassing for William and may have helped to turn his thoughts towards parliamentary union between his kingdoms.

Meanwhile, Scotland's aspirations to become a colonial power in her own right had a worrying potential to cut across English foreign policy. For their part, the Scots were incensed when England failed to support them – as was the case with the Darien Scheme of 1698–1700, when Scotland tried to colonise land in Panama that was already within the Spanish Empire. A series of English Parliamentary laws known as the Navigation Acts already excluded Scots from imperial trade. Effectively Scotland was being treated as a foreign state, but not permitted to act like one.

Many Scots wanted to see the Stuart line return to the throne in the person of James VIII, the child born in 1688, who since 1701 had been the nominal heir-in-exile. The English Parliament excluded him through an Act of Succession on which the Scottish Parliament was never consulted. It was assumed Scotland would fall into line. It did not, and although the Scottish Parliament of the first years of Queen Anne (r. 1702–14) did not go so far as to back the return of her half-brother to the throne, an anxious English governing class viewed its activities with alarm. In 1703 the 'Act anent Peace and War' stipulated that no future monarch could lead Scotland into war without the consent of the Scottish Parliament. This raised the prospect of a separate Scottish foreign policy re-emerging – even a renewed French alliance.

Impoverished by war, yet restless, globally ambitious and a worsening irritant – perhaps even a genuine threat – to English interests, Scotland was treating the composite monarchy as if it involved equal partners with equal say. This was not an easy state of affairs.

CHAPTER 4

UNION AND EMPIRE

Scotland in 1707 was an impoverished state, weakened by almost a century of intermittent conflict and futile attempts to secure a role on the world stage. Its resources were further depleted by poor harvests and the effects of climate change. These failings had disrupted the country's traditional elites, who were in any case increasingly divided on sectarian lines. At one end of the spectrum were hardline ideological Presbyterians who favoured Union with England; at the other were Episcopalian and Catholic Jacobites ready to take up arms against England and their Scottish peers.

Leading lights at both ends of the spectrum had been hit hard by the Darien disaster, the strategically brilliant but operationally impossible attempt to create a Scottish colony near the present location of the Panama Canal, in the backyard of the powerful Spanish Empire. The Company of Scotland had 3,000 shareholders for the venture, which ended in the deaths of many settlers and bankruptcy for many members of the elite. One consequence was to make Scotland even more vulnerable to Union.

State of the Union

After the Revolution of 1688–91 and the deposition and exile of the Stuart King James (VII of Scotland, II of England), who was notably sympathetic to Scottish concerns, English government opinion moved in favour of political union with Scotland. The Scottish Estates resisted the English Act of Settlement of 1701, which settled the succession on the German House of Hanover (Queen Anne having no heir). In 1705 the English government took a more decisive step, demanding an incorporating Union. This would effectively merge the two countries – or rather absorb Scotland into England, preventing it from forming its own alliance with the French (with whom England was at war for all but six years between 1689 and 1714) or with the Dutch (with whom England had fought three wars from 1660 to 1688). A Union with Scotland would not only safeguard England from its chief European rivals but also enable it to project power more effectively overseas. As one Scottish historian has memorably put it, it would be a Union for Empire.

Some of the Scots elite favoured the idea. Others recognised that the political situation of Scotland would have to change in any case, but mooted alternatives: a confederal arrangement with the Netherlands, perhaps, or some sort of federal union with England. Still others opposed it altogether. Among the population as a whole, outright opposition was by far the most common stance. The Union enjoyed no popular mandate – and, crucially, the exiled Stuart dynasty were against it.

The issue provoked strong emotions across Scotland and unleashed a ferocious pamphlet war in 1705–6. By this time Union with England had already been agreed in principle, with its precise form being determined by the Scottish Estates and Union Commissioners. These had been selected in the Crown's interest and were largely biddable; certainly, many ordinary Scots did not see them as their legitimate representatives. By contrast, the Convention of Royal Burghs voted to oppose the Union and thirty-seven shires and royal burghs also petitioned against it. Tens of thousands of signatures supported the petitions and others like it. Many protested that the Union was unconstitutional. One writer called for a national assembly of men and women to debate the measure, declaring 'Fundamental National Rights' common to both sexes; others called for a guarantee that Scottish parliamentary consent would be needed for English foreign policy.

It is estimated that three-quarters of the anti-Union population favoured a return of the exiled King James VIII. These Jacobites – the name given to supporters of James and his descendants – would become the chief vehicle for the restoration of Scottish independence. Over the following years, the Jacobite cause was to leave a deep mark on Scottish and British history.

Meanwhile, feelings were running dangerously high and concessions were made to dampen the risk of revolt. The place of the Presbyterian Kirk in post-Union Scotland would be protected, and the Scottish crown jewels (the 'Honours of Scotland') would remain in the northern kingdom. In the end the Union ratified by the Scottish Estates on 16 January 1707 was a curiously hybrid document: both a treaty between two sovereign nations and an act of two parliaments by which one of them extinguished its own existence.

There were contemporary accusations of bribery: a waggish poster appeared in late 1706 advertising Scotland for sale at public auction at Scone, the ancient crowning place of Scottish kings. The reserve price was set at £400,000 – the compensation offered to Scotland for taking on her share of the English national debt. The Union brought a general increase in taxation – and English officers came north to enforce it. They were greeted by passive resistance as well as more forthright attacks.

The Union

The Union is a tricky document to parse. It simultaneously talks about 'that part of the United Kingdom now called Scotland' and of a 'Kingdom of Scotland' that remains a separate jurisdiction in respect of religious, legal, official and institutional rights. The Union conceives of a 'United Kingdoms' (at that time sometimes plural), over which parliamentary rights are sovereign, yet preserves the Crown's own continuing rights in the Kingdom of Scotland.

The document's key clauses are Article II, which enforces the Act of Settlement and the Hanoverian succession in Scotland; Articles IV, VI and VII, which address freedom of trade (particularly overseas) and a customs union; and Articles X–XIII and XVI–XVII, which give Westminster sovereignty over tax and prescribe the standardisation of the currency as well as weights and measures (although these did not in fact come in until the 1820s). Articles XVIII and XIX preserve Scots law and legal system, but with some UK oversight.

Despite the fact that there was to be one Great Britain (Article I), the Great Seal of Scotland was to be retained (Article XXIV) in respect of rights confined within 'the kingdom' [i.e. of Scotland]. More than three hundred years on, the Union remains an extraordinarily complex and fascinating document.

Queen Anne ordered an official copy of the act to be sent to Scotland. This copy, known as the Exemplification of the Act of Union, is dated 7 March 1707. The document is illustrated with a portrait of Anne and assorted symbols of both Scotland and England, such as the unicorn and the lion.

The Jacobite Cause

The Jacobites had failed to scupper the Union, but in 1708 France supported a Jacobite Rising. This failed to come off due to swift action by the Royal Navy, which headed off the French expedition. Although the French declined to respond to the Jacobite call to arms in 1715 – largely due to internal politics – the desire to divide England from Scotland and Ireland remained a constant of French foreign policy throughout the eighteenth century. England's Jacobite problem was thus also its French problem. All the Risings up to and including 1746 had ending the Anglo-Scottish Union as one of their key political goals, along with restoring the Stuart dynasty.

The struggle to bring back James and the Stuarts to the throne of Scotland remained a central feature of the Scottish political landscape until the middle of the eighteenth century. In England, the Jacobite cause was associated with religious conservatism and a xenophobic tilt against a Dutch (William), then German (the Havoverian Georges) monarchy. In Scotland and Ireland, support for the Jacobites was tied to a range of national grievances and the goal of restoring the Stuart composite monarchy in full, with strong national parliaments and inbuilt protection for Catholicism in Ireland and Episcopalianism in Scotland.

Tartan and a wide range of coded elements in visual and material culture acted as symbols of Jacobitism – the Edinburgh Pattern of tartan introduced in 1713 was explicitly Jacobite. Institutions such as the Royal Company of Archers and at least some of the Scottish Rite freemason lodges acted as Jacobite fronts. Books and pamphlets published by closet pro-Jacobite houses dropped allusions to Mary Queen of Scots, William Wallace, Robert Bruce and the Wars of Independence.

Across Europe, Jacobite networks continued to support and patronise Scots. A cadre of Jacobite soldiery, exiled for political or religious reasons from Scotland, formed across the Continent: the Austrian generals James Lockhart and James Wishart, the Prussian Field Marshal James Keith, the Russian admiral Thomas Gordon, the Venetian Colonel Livingston and many others. Scots in Rome such as David Wemyss, Lord Elcho, gathered together with fellow Jacobites to play and sing Scots songs – especially on St Andrew's Day, 30 November. The themes of exile and homesickness characteristic of Scots song seem to have become popular at this time, leaving a lasting legacy – most famously, perhaps, in 'Auld Lang Syne', with its images of wandering and overseas exile.

The 1715 Rebellion

In 1715, around 21,000 men rose in Scotland to restore the Stuarts and end the Union, with a supporting force of 1,000 from northern England. The commander of this rising was John Erskine, 6th Earl of Mar, who was a politician and not a military leader. Despite his grand, oft-stated objective – to break the Union by fighting in the cause of Scotland's ancient liberties – Mar was unable to cope with the scale of the troops at his disposal. His procrastination and poor leadership led to a division of his forces, and he failed to follow up his advantage at the Battle of Sheriffmuir in November 1715. There was no formal French support, and James – who had not authorised Mar's raising of the royal standard – only landed in Peterhead when the Rising was already on the wane. It would shortly be over altogether.

James Francis Edward Stuart lands at Peterhead, 1715

> His Lordship told me that he was instructed and ordered by King James as soon as possible to Emit and Publish a declaration against the UNION ... most of the Nobility and Gentry ... Concur in their Zeal and Resolution against the UNION ... I pray God blesse all their honest designs with Successe.
>
> A Letter from a Gentleman in the Earl of Mar's Camp (1715)

Although some estates were confiscated after 1715 and many Jacobite teachers, magistrates and other officials dismissed, government efforts to suppress Jacobitism in Scotland met with limited success. Geography once again hindered progress. Between 1726 and 1738, British troops under the command of General George Wade built forty bridges and 400 kilometres of road to make northern Scotland more accessible. Yet many of the large estates, though nominally in the hands of Scottish elites loyal to the British Crown, continued to supply the Jacobites with manpower when it was needed.

The 1745 Rebellion

On 23 December 1743, James VIII (the 'Old Pretender' to his opponents, whose propaganda claimed he was illegitimate) declared against the 'pretended Union' which had reduced Scotland, 'a Nation always famous for valour ... to the condition of a Province'. In August 1745, another campaign was launched at Glenfinnan, with the royal standard of the House of Stuart raised to the cries of 'King James the Eight ... prosperity to Scotland and no Union'. The Jacobite Rising of 1745 was the last major challenge of the British imperial era from a European-aligned Scotland.

When he landed in Montrose with Scottish and Irish troops in the French service in November 1745, Lord John Drummond took care to announce that he came on behalf of James's son Charles, 'Regent of SCOTLAND' to make war against the 'King of ENGLAND'. At the Treaty of Fontainebleau in October, Louis XV had committed France to supporting the Jacobite effort, and Voltaire – himself a Jacobite sympathiser – was contracted to write the manifesto for the French invasion force.

'Lost portrait' of Charles Edward Stuart ('Bonnie Prince Charlie') by Allan Ramsay

Within weeks, Charles' commanders were astonished to find themselves in striking distance of London without having fought a major battle in England. France was on the point of sending further troops, with some eighteen infantry battalions and nine cavalry squadrons in preparation.

The gains were soon squandered. The odds against Jacobite success had always been long, but defeat became certain at Derby in December, when Charles's commanders lost their nerve and withdrew. Despite a tactical victory at Clifton and a more substantial win at Falkirk in January 1746, dwindling resources and failing morale, combined with internal differences among the prince and his commanders, led to further retreat. The abandonment of Scotland's east coast ports made French reinforcement more difficult. Final defeat by George II's son, the Duke of Cumberland, came at Culloden in April 1746, as the Jacobites tried to halt the British advance on Inverness, the last major burgh they controlled.

Culloden: An End to the Auld Alliance

When French regulars stood on Culloden Moor on 16 April 1746 to fight for the Stuart Prince Charles and an end to the Anglo-Scottish Union, it marked the last stand in a long, united struggle by the French and Scottish crowns against a mutual English foe. The final symbolic feint was Captain du Saussay's heroic artillery defence on the Jacobite left, which helped prevent the encirclement of Charles' army by British dragoon and horse regiments.

In more recent years, the captain's home of Château du Saussay in Essone has been used to film both *The Day of the Jackal* (1973) and *Dangerous Liaisons* (1988). Both dramas are tame compared with the carnage on that final day of the Auld Alliance in Scotland, when the Jacobite army was crushed. Between 1560 and 1746, Scotland had experienced a greater range of foreign liaisons, dangerous and otherwise, than at any earlier time in its history. Had the union between Scotland and France survived, it would have likely changed Scottish history every bit as much as the regnal (1603) and parliamentary (1707) unions with England did.

Medal commemorating British victory at Culloden, 1746

Jacobite defeat set the stage for many changes, not least the influx of large numbers of Scots into the British Army. From this time onwards, Scottish troops played a critical role in imperial campaigns, as in the Seven Years War of 1756–63, giving rise to the martial myth of the Scottish soldier in the British Empire. After Culloden, Cumberland and his supporters had proposed several radical measures, among them depopulating parts of Scotland, transporting their inhabitants to the West Indies and colonising the country with foreign Protestants. All of these were seen as too extreme by the British government, conscious that since the Union, Scotland was part of the state rather than a colony. Further afield, fewer qualms were on display: some 14,000 French Canadians were expelled from Nova Scotia and neighbouring territories in 1755–7, and Continental European Protestants were deployed as settlers and soldiers in North America. Final Jacobite defeat in 1745 thus crystallised aspects of British imperial policy abroad, enhancing the reputation of the army and strengthening the Empire's ability to project military force.

What If the Jacobites Had Won?

Not all the possible outcomes of a Jacobite victory would have come to pass, but understanding what was at stake is vital if we want to grasp the significance and scope of what was a truly international movement.

1. Great Britain might have become a three-kingdom state rather than a centralised one: a fully composite monarchy with a restored Scottish Parliament and Scotland free to trade and colonise overseas; an Irish Parliament which was less – if at all – subsidiary to England's (as James II's last Irish

Parliament of 1689 made clear); and a Crown that was aware that many of its strongest supporters lay outside the English south-east. At this time, it should be remembered, the combined population of Scotland and Ireland was not far short of that of England.

2. On the global front, imperial competition with France would have been less intense. The Seven Years' War (1756–63), in which a million died and France suffered comprehensive defeat, might well have been avoided. In turn, the American colonies would have been more wary of rebelling in the face of an undefeated France with its American possessions intact. This wealthier, less economically and militarily over-stretched France could then have redirected resources internally, potentially saving European monarchies from the French Revolution and Napoleon Bonaparte – and with longer-term consequences for the creation of German and Italian statehood and the conflicts of the twentieth century.

The British governments of the time were in no doubt: Jacobite success would serve France's interests across the globe. Yet in French eyes at least, the world of the restored Stuarts would be bipolar, with the two leading global powers – the British composite monarchy and France – no longer locked in a zero-sum game for sole ascendancy. The dream of a European Scotland – Queen Mary's Scotland – and the prospect of a looser, less Francophobe British polity both ended at Culloden, the last battle for a Continental as opposed to an imperial Scotland.

Scotland Within the Union

The Great Britain which Scotland joined with the Union was already a highly centralised state. For all that, Scotland remained very much a distinct society throughout the eighteenth century. Its separate legal system kept it a jurisdiction in its own right and not merely a part of Britain (as had been recognised in the ambivalence of the Union settlement). Scottish institutions such as the Faculty of Advocates, the College of Justice, the Kirk, the banks, the schools and the universities all remained autonomous. It was largely thanks to its deep historical ties with the established Church that the education system stayed independent under the Union.

The widespread official patronage system in Scotland also survived. Much Scottish business was controlled or influenced by wealthy magnates: it has been estimated that the 3rd Duke of Argyll and 1st Earl of Ilay (1682–1761) was alone responsible for thousands of appointments through private preferment. Unlike most elements of Scottish society, the upper nobility was integrated into Great Britain at an early stage. The lesser nobility, the professional, mercantile and burgess classes and the tradespeople and farmers all continued to be linked by Scottish networks of kinship, location and institution.

With traditional paths to advancement such as the law still open, along with newer opportunities in medicine and other professions, members of the lesser nobility came to form what might be called a professional aristocracy in Scotland. Certain families came to dominate the upper ranks of individual professions across the centuries. Perhaps the classic example is the Dundas family, whose star had risen a few generations earlier. Sir James Dundas of Arniston (1620–79) was a Lord of Session, one of Scotland's most senior judges, and his son-in-law the Comptroller of the Exchequer. Robert Dundas (1650–1726) was also a Lord of Session, while his son Robert (1685–1753) was Lord President, Scotland's most senior judge. Robert Dundas (1713–87) was Solicitor General, then Lord Advocate and then Lord President; Robert Dundas (1758–1819) was Solicitor General, Lord Advocate and Chief Baron of the Exchequer. Henry Dundas (1742–1811) was Solicitor General, Lord Advocate, Dean of the Faculty of Advocates, a British Cabinet Minister and 1st Viscount Melville. His son Robert Dundas (1771–1851) held the senior legal position of Keeper of the Signet. Between 1690 and 1730, around a third of new advocates were the sons of peers or baronets, and in a similar period some 90 per cent of advocates promoted to the Scottish bench were educated abroad as well as in Scotland. Academic dynasties also entrenched themselves, with professorships being handed from father to son.

Long after the Union, Scotland continued to train and export its native elites. As the Enlightenment dawned, certain schools and universities grew powerful networks of their own, reinforced by the civic mercantile culture of the cities and towns in which they were based: a mutual bond of business, education and the professions served to promote the interests of Scots worldwide.

Northern Lights

The Scottish Enlightenment was distinctively Enlightened, in that it applied reason to knowledge; and distinctively Scottish, in that it did so in service of material and not merely intellectual improvement (perhaps not surprising, given the country's relative poverty by the late seventeenth century).

From the beginning, the Enlightenment was closely associated with practical aims such as accurate measurement.

Improved clocks divided the day into ever-narrower segments of time, and watches were widely adopted as personal timepieces. Other trends include attempts to standardise local weights and measures; the introduction of consistently milled rather than erratically hammered coinage (1662); the mass production of standardised glass and ceramic wares; and even the emergence of a regular annual fashion season. The housing and art markets also emerged in this period, as well as street lighting, libraries, coach timetables and a postal service. Even as taxonomical order was imposed on the world of things, so too was intellectual order brought to the world of human ideas. A plethora of clubs and societies mediated between these two worlds, such as the Musical Society or the later Select Society of Edinburgh.

Edinburgh was the leading light of the Scottish Enlightenment. Its wealth, dominant trading position, mix of residential and commercial property, and compact size – the core city, home to almost 30,000 people, covered less than a square kilometre – fostered innovation. So too did the city's role as a seat of government and national professional institutions, and the highly educated citizens that peopled them.

As a major trading city, Edinburgh was diverse. Small but important French and Dutch communities were engaged in jewellery, paper-making, japanning and other trades. Around 20–25 per cent of its merchants were involved in foreign trade, and a high proportion of the local elite were educated abroad and had absorbed outside ideas. At home, Scotland's higher education sector was much cheaper and accessible to a wider range of people than its English counterpart. The Scottish university curriculum moved rapidly to embrace the scientific revolution and Copernican and Cartesian ideas about the solar system and consciousness.

In terms of gender, too, Edinburgh was relatively open. The city trades recognised women burgesses. Women could divorce in Scotland – there were cheap fixed fees for this, as well as limited free advice from legal and medical professional bodies and even the provision of pensions by the city. Wives could be named in causes for debt before the courts. In the seventeenth century, 36 per cent of burgh court debt cases involved a female creditor and 34 per cent a female debtor.

Eighty per cent of Dutch trade to the whole country came into the Forth and 63 per cent of Scotland's French wine imports came into Leith. As a whole, Edinburgh was responsible for between a third and two-fifths of the country's economy.

A postal service, newspapers and early libraries had all emerged by the end of the seventeenth century. As early as 1658, a library was established for the Royal High School, while what is now the National Library of Scotland was founded as the Advocates' Library in 1681–2. There were also huge private libraries in the hands of pioneering thinkers such as Andrew Fletcher of Saltoun (1653–1716), Archibald Pitcairne (1652–1713) and Sir Andrew Balfour (1630–94). In 1725, Allan Ramsay (1684–1758) founded in Edinburgh what has been identified as the first subscription library in the British Isles. Free libraries were also set up at Haddington (1729) and elsewhere. The key Enlightenment practice of reading spread far beyond the elites and crossed class and gender boundaries: there were even libraries in inns.

Edinburgh's (now Royal) Botanic Garden was founded in 1670 and became deeply integrated with the university medical faculty's research and, still more importantly, training programme. Other universities in Scotland followed suit, helping to underwrite the significant Scottish contribution to botany across the British Empire.

Both Charles II and James VII sponsored extensive building in the Scottish capital and supported civic redevelopment. What eventually became the New Town in Edinburgh was first envisioned under James, who helped found many other institutions that underpinned the Enlightenment in Scotland: the Royal College of Physicians of Edinburgh (1681), the Edinburgh Merchant Company (1681), the Advocates' Library (1682) and the Order of the Thistle (1687), as well as the offices of Historiographer and Geographer Royal (1681–2).

In the wake of Union, a wealth of new institutions affirmed Edinburgh's capital status, such as Allan Ramsay's theatre (1736) and the Academy of St Luke, Scotland's first art school (1729). Clubs and associations for improvement of all kinds were formed, such as the Honourable Society of Improvers in the Knowledge of Agriculture in Scotland (1723), the Society for the Improvement of Medical Knowledge (1731) and the Philosophical Society (1737).

Statue of Adam Smith in Edinburgh

This dynamic city was the birthplace of some of the most innovative ideas of the eighteenth century. David Hume (1711–76) pursued a science of human nature; his radically sceptical take on the possibility of absolute knowledge has never been surpassed. John Law (1671–1729) devised modern fiat currency (while acting as Comptroller General of the finances of France). James Hutton (1726–97) founded the science of geology that made Darwin's ideas possible. William Robertson (1721–93) became arguably the first global and the first anti-colonial historian. Adam Ferguson (1723–1816) founded sociology. Mary Somerville (1780–1872), polymath and supporter of female suffrage, expanded the horizon of possibilities for women.

The city of Glasgow enjoyed many of the same advantages as Edinburgh, with a similarly high quality of education and a desire for improvement. Francis Hutcheson (1694–1746) explored the role of sympathy in morality; Adam Smith (1723–90) founded modern economics and (arguably) the modern approach to history, and made links between human co-operation, sympathy, business and trade; John Anderson (1726–96) championed the opening of higher education to women and the working class; while Thomas Reid (1710–96) countered Hume's scepticism with a globally important definition of 'common sense' as the basis for rationality.

A conversation between Anderson and James Watt (1736–1819) about the limitations of their erstwhile colleague Joseph Black's steam condenser in Glasgow is believed to have led to Watt's world-changing innovation in steam power. The Hunter brothers, John and William, pioneered modern surgery and anatomy as well as creating perhaps the first collection based on the scientific principles of Enlightenment, which as the Hunterian became Scotland's first public museum in 1807.

Prospects Dreary

While distinguishing itself intellectually, Scotland remained far poorer than England financially, culturally and agriculturally. The growing population in the north of the country put pressure on the land: by 1650 there were only 1.2–1.6 hectares of arable land per family – very low in European terms. The meagre and scattered distribution of property was aggravated by the practice of partible inheritance: that is, dividing estates among the heirs after a landowner's death. By the late eighteenth century, the average was down to just one hectare per head. Large-scale farming was culturally alien in many parts of Scotland, and the move away from rent-in-kind to cash rents was a slow one. In 1723, the Honourable Society of Improvers in the Knowledge of Agriculture in Scotland began to champion the creation of sizeable estates (such as in forestry) and planned villages. The pressure to improve and develop land led to its enclosure in the south; in the north, the preference of rural communities for small and partible holdings proved more entrenched.

It was around this time that the lengthy Scottish or 'Highland' Clearances began. External economic shocks, demand for cash rents, the desire of landowners to improve the land and raise income, and the inability of many tenants to sustain their smallholdings – many had no access to common land for grazing or fuel – combined to create an economic crisis that lasted for 150 years. Land use changed extensively. In the north, vast tracts were given over to the grazing of sheep, and later to forest for deer. Removed from the land by force, persuasion or necessity, many rural Scots emigrated to Scotland's cities, or abroad to North America, Australia or New Zealand.

Meanwhile, Enlightened attempts to unify Scottish and English standards progressed in fits and starts. Under the terms of the 1707 Union, Scotland's currency was officially merged into sterling at the slightly advantageous exchange rate of 12:1, but it remained a unit of account into the nineteenth century and sometimes beyond – a sheriff issued a fine of 100 Scots merks as late as 1931, and linguistic terms such as 'bawbee' for sixpence survived well into the twentieth century. Standardised weights and measures were not introduced formally into Scotland until the 1820s, before which both Dutch and local measures remained widespread. Confusingly, English and Scottish units might share the same name but represent a different length or breadth. The 'Royal Mile' in Edinburgh, for example, is a Scots mile of 5,952 feet, considerably longer than the English mile at 5,280 feet; acres in Scotland were 26 per cent larger than their English equivalent.

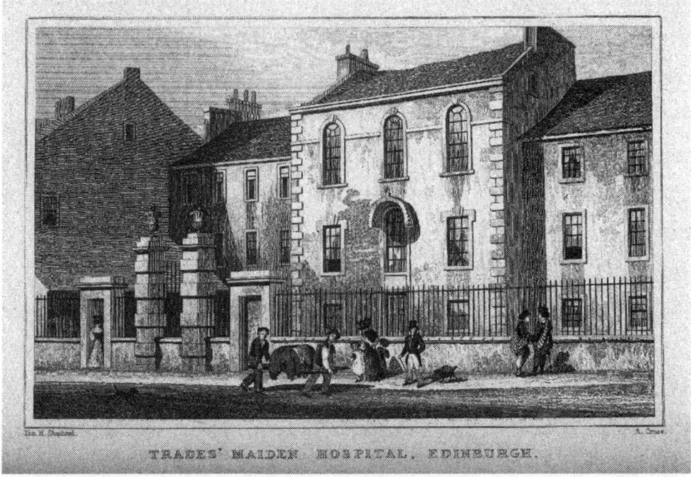

The Merchant Maiden Hospital

Women played a highly visible role in Scottish business and other walks of life. By the late seventeenth century there were numerous female merchants in Scotland – 400 female exporters in total, a far higher ratio per capita than in London.

Dozens more were active in Scottish trading concerns in Europe in locations such as Rotterdam. There were institutions to educate women in Aberdeen and in Edinburgh, where the Merchant Maiden Hospital, established in 1694, endures today as the Mary Erskine School.

The new Union taxes made smuggling a popular crime, as well as a highly politicised one. As late as the 1740s, the total value of smuggled goods was almost a quarter of legal imports. It has been estimated that duty was paid on less than 2 per cent of French wine imported into Scotland, while at the beginning of the century over half of tobacco was shipped by smugglers. Some ships specialised in particular types of contraband: the *Charlotte* of Peterhead was a notorious carrier of spirits. British excise taxes were seen as unjust by many – particularly in the east, where relative economic decline fed a natural tendency to Jacobitism among largely Episcopalian communities, and smugglers often carried French agents and Jacobite propaganda. By contrast, the west coast of Scotland, which faced the Caribbean and America's Atlantic seaboard, gained more from the Union. By 1747, Glasgow had cornered 50 per cent of all British tobacco exports to France; this had risen to 60 per cent by 1751.

In music, literature and art, the idea of a distinct, native Scottish tradition evolved and was even reinforced after the Union. The poet and cultural entrepreneur Allan Ramsay set out to make song and poetry in the Scots language respectable throughout the Anglophone world. Meanwhile the Scottish art market shifted from the Netherlands towards the Italian states, not least because of the presence there of King James VIII's court in exile at Urbino (1717–21) and then Rome (1721–66). In Edinburgh Italian composers hybridised Scottish tunes with their own airs.

Scotland's distinct environment, the relative diversity of Edinburgh's population, the cosmopolitanism of its professional and educated classes, and a revival of interest in native traditions helped to crystallise a cultural identity that had already been brought into sharp focus by England's political ascendancy. All these forces acted in different ways to produce the Scottish Enlightenment and the global cultural legacy of Jacobitism. As Scotland came to assume an ever more important role in the imperial British project, both movements acquired a distinctly international outlook.

Scotland Abroad

Faced with the thorny problem of how to secure Scotland within the Union, Sir Robert Walpole (1676–1745), arguably Great Britain's first and certainly its longest-serving prime minister, promoted Scottish involvement in the British Empire, particularly in India. The aim was to integrate the country more closely and to imbue it with a common sense of purpose. Scots took full advantage of the opportunity. There was a long-standing tradition of Scottish travel and trade abroad, and the lure of success in the professions attracted impoverished nobles. Moreover, there was an over-supply of educated Scotsmen relative to the number of opportunities available to them at home. Between 1720 and 1757, Scots made up all the principal medical officers in Madras/Chennai. By the 1780s, Scots comprised around half of the writers, officers and assistant surgeons in Bengal.

Scots were also making rapid progress in North America, not least via land grants to soldiers after the end of the Seven Years War (1756–63), as well as in the slavery-dependent colonies of the Caribbean. By 1754, 25 per cent of Jamaican land was in Scottish hands, while 60 per cent of doctors on Antigua were

Scots-trained. Up to half of the European settlers in Jamaica and 80 per cent of those in Antigua were Scots by the latter part of the eighteenth century. Slaves in the Caribbean called shellfish 'Scotsmen', perhaps owing to their habit of clinging together. Although the slave trade generally did not pass through Scottish ports, Scots played a major role in British slave trading – and indeed traded directly from Africa. Grant, Oswald & Co. commenced operations on Bance Island in 1748: 13,000 Africans were shipped from Bance into chattel slavery. The Grant/Oswald consortium also gained the contracts to supply food to British forces during the 1756–63 war in North America, where other Scots, Jacobite exiles prominent among them, were engendering a dynasty of Native American chiefs.

Lachlan MacGillivray (1718–99), one of the original colonists of Georgia in the 1730s, was the ancestor of a number of these chiefs. He married the Creek noblewoman Sehoy Marchand of the Wind Clan, and his son Alexander MacGillivray (*Hoboi-Hili-Miko*, 'Good Child King', 1750–93) became a Creek chief who played off America against Spain. Childhood stories about Culloden made him fear that Native Americans – with whom Highlanders were often compared – could be next.

Lachlan MacGillivray's other descendants included William Weatherford and Peter McQueen (*c.* 1780–1820), who led the brutal American Indian attack on American settlers at Fort Mims in Alabama in 1813. William Macintosh (*Tustunnuggee Hutke*, White Warrior, 1775–1825) likewise became a Creek chief, though an unsuccessful one, while Hugh Monroe (1798–1892) married the daughter of a Blackfeet chief and John Macdonnel, son of a Jacobite exile, led dozens of raids in the service of Thayendanegea, the Mohawk military leader. John Ross (1790–1866), *kooseskowe*

(Little White Bird), paramount chief of the Cherokee, led his people on the Trail of Tears to Oklahoma. There were many different kinds of Scots in British North America.

The house at Rossville, Georgia, built by John Ross, Paramount Chief of the Cherokee. He lived here until 1832.

Tartan

Today, tartan is the most visible sign of Scottishness. Originally its different 'setts' or patterns signified particular locations and affiliations, or sometimes families or clans–though this did not become codified until the nineteenth century. Tartan setts were usually associated with the north of the country, and as such were worn by the Scottish royal family. Later tartan became popular as a patriotic marker of Stuart and Jacobite loyalty, which in turn led to its suppression in perceived Jacobite areas after 1746.

In the British Army, meanwhile, the use of tartan was legitimised, as it was gradually co-opted for shows of British rather than Scottish patriotism. After the repeal of legislation banning its use in 1782, military tartan filtered back into civil society. It was around this time that The Highland Society of London began to codify the use of family tartans. By the 1790s, William Wilson and Sons of Bannockburn was plying a lucrative trade in civilian setts.

In 1789, Prince George (the future George IV) wore tartan at a masquerade ball for the first time. By the royal visit to Edinburgh in 1822, tartan had become a badge of Hanoverian – as once of Stuart – loyalty to the Crown. The pattern was also spilling beyond Scottish borders, with periodic appearances in French fashion and even on Qing porcelain.

In the British Empire's overseas territories, tartan was worn above all as a marker of Scottish ethnicity, but 'Universal' tartans such Black Watch or Royal Stewart could be worn by anyone wishing to display sympathy with Scots and Scotland. First Nations chiefs received tartan as a gift, and their people donned it: tartan shawls were a particular favourite among the Cree. New tartans proliferated throughout the Americas – at Fort Vancouver alone, some two miles of tartan were sold in 1849.

If Scotland's symbols were beginning to travel the world, at home forces of dislocation were at work. The armies which fought the European wars of 1756–63 and 1793–1815, in which thousands of men from northern Scotland died, had often depended on small grants of land to attract recruits. Many formerly landless men returned as veterans to these smallholdings, crofts carved out of marginal land or that of displaced subtenants. By 1820, smaller crofts predominated over communal land use. They were often barely sustainable. As it became less feasible to provide tenants with a smallholding in exchange for their labour, the numbers of day workers rose, and estate villages grew up to house them.

The economic downturn that followed the end of the Napoleonic Wars (1799–1815) intensified pressures, with sheep replacing people on much of the land in the northern counties. Even as remaining smallholders struggled to pay rents, noble landlords sought to squeeze more income from their estates to boost their status in British society. Evicted and displaced people in their turn put pressure on townships, and the return of demobbed soldiers after 1815 further impacted living conditions in the cities – as did the 'year without a summer' in 1816 that followed the Tambora volcanic eruption in what is today Indonesia.

As in Ireland, many smallholders emigrated in the face of intolerable economic duress – a process often referred to, from the 1880s at least, as the 'Highland Clearances'. These were not a single great eviction but a long-running process of agricultural dispossession, in which first sheep then deer played the catalyst for human expulsions. Shabby treatment of rural Scots was justified by the 'scientific racism' of the nineteenth century, which blamed Scotland's economic failings on the indolence of the Celt in contrast to the industrious Saxon. In the end, the Napier Commission of 1883–84 – a public inquiry into the condition of the crofting counties of the north – gave rise to the Crofters' Holdings (Scotland) Act of 1886, which established fair rents, security of tenure and compensation for improvements.

Despite these disruptions, political radicalism remained a relatively marginal phenomenon in Scotland. There were many reasons for this, but the country's heavy investment in the Napoleonic Wars and extensive repatriation of money from the Empire (especially India) to Scotland brought benefit and comfort to many in the cities, which may have lessened the appeal of radical politics. In 1820, however, after the Peterloo massacre of English radicals the previous year, there was a major strike and a small-scale Scottish insurrection. A provisional government was declared, making reference to Magna Carta and the Bill of Rights – notably English Whig points of reference, though today the 1820 'Rising' is mythologised in some Scottish nationalist circles.

Volatile trade swings after the Napoleonic Wars added to the numbers of those displaced and physically or economically damaged by war or misfortune. Yet ordinary criminality remained a more serious threat than political insurrection; Glasgow formed the first regular police force in the United Kingdom in 1800. Nationalism in Scotland tended to be a cultural affair, promoting the country's history and heritage while steering clear of a transformative political agenda. This position is sometimes termed 'Unionist Nationalism'.

Even so, the centralisation of Great Britain in the era was seen by some as an assault on the Union settlement. The introduction of the English system of lords lieutenant in 1794, the abolition of Scottish revenue commissioners in 1823, the adoption of imperial measures in 1824–26, the management of Scotland by the Home Office from 1827 and the abolition of the Admiralty Court (1830), the Scottish Board of Customs and Excise (1843) and other institutions all diminished Scotland's status within the Union. These changes triggered calls to recognise the Union as a more balanced partnership, and paved the way for later organisations such as the National Association for the Vindication of Scottish Rights (NAVSR, founded 1853).

In the 1750s, 51 per cent of Scotland's population lived north of the Tay and around 37 per cent inhabited the central lowlands. By 1821, the balance was changing fast, with a shift of people to the central belt, and within that to the west. The country was industrialising at speed: by the early-to-mid nineteenth century, a quarter of all pig-iron and 25 per cent of the wool of Great Britain and Ireland was produced by Scotland. The work of James Watt (1736–1819) in steam, William Murdoch (1754–1839) in gas lighting and James Nelson's (1792–1865) blast furnace left a Scottish mark on many major industrial processes.

In 1812, the first passenger steamboat service in Europe was launched from Glasgow in the shape of Henry Bell's *Comet*. A raft of innovations put Scottish entrepreneurs at the forefront of global economic growth from the 1840s, partly on the back of capital derived from India and the Caribbean. James Harrison's invention of the refrigerator in the following decade helped make exports of perishable foods possible. In medicine, James Young Simpson with chloroform (1847), Alexander Wood with the hypodermic syringe (1853) and Joseph Lister with antiseptic procedure (1865–67) all extended the bounds of surgical possibility.

James Harrison's patented ice-making machine

Burns and Bagpipes: Scotland the Brand

At the very moment that Scottish inventors and businessmen were preparing the ground for the economic rebirth of the nineteenth century, Scotland's Romantic poets and artists were laying down a national legacy of a different kind.

To celebrate the nation's heroic past, Scottish Romantic artists created a national taxonomy of glory. Their distinctive and highly selective blend of fact and fantasy soon spread beyond Scottish borders to become a powerful international brand. There were two main reasons for this. The first was the global appeal of Scottish writers such as James Macpherson (1736–96), Robert Burns (1759–96), Sir Walter Scott (1771–1832) and George Gordon, Lord Byron (1788–1824). The second was the physical geography of Scotland itself, the inaccessible and dramatic Highland landscape that had once harboured the greatest internal threat faced by the British Empire, but then became both inspiration and resource for Great Britain's global military power – and an exotic destination for package tourists from the south.

An archetypal Scottish 'Highland' landscape: *Glencoe* by Waller Hugh Paton

To many across the world, Scotland remains today what it became then in the popular mind: a rural, rugged country of mountain and flood, bagpipes and tartan, clan castles and conflict, whisky and golf, ghosts and ghost-seers. This Scotland is a product of Scottish Romanticism, globally distributed by poem, pamphlet, novel and song.

An episode from James Macpherson's Ossian poems, showing Fingal as he arrives at the cave of Turthor. Engraving by Alexander Runciman, 1772–3

James Macpherson, born into a Jacobite family, produced a Scottish epic of defeat and loss about the legendary Gaelic hero Fingal (*Fionn mac Cumhaill*). Published as if written by Fionn's son Ossian, it was in fact collated and heavily adapted from Gaelic sources. Macpherson was not – as scholars with no Gaelic have often claimed – a forger or a faker, but a restorer (albeit one who took significant liberties with his sources). The Ossian poems, melding the directness of Homeric epic with a civilised Enlightenment sensibility, were widely translated. Friedrich Wilhelm Rust (1739–96) was the first to set them to music; over 300 Ossian-inspired compositions would follow.

Macpherson's polite representation of primitive violence spoke to the public mood of mourning and military remembrance following the million dead of the Seven Years War. The Ossian poems became a source of inspiration across Europe: epics of national identity were composed in Finland (the *Kalevala*, 1835), the Netherlands, Poland, Slovenia and other nations. Visitors flocked to see the country of Fingal, and he even acquired a cave on Staffa in 1774, as well as a 'Hall' in Perthshire (at the Hermitage, off the A9) nine years later. By 1830, when Felix Mendelssohn (1809–47) composed his concert overture *The Hebrides* – soon given the title *Fingal's Cave* – Ossian had become central to the idea of Scotland in the European imagination.

Burns and Scott did even more than Macpherson to put Scotland on the global map. Burns' poetry and song expressed a deep and universal humanity born out of Enlightenment values. Radical in tone and allusion, it was nevertheless often hard to pin down politically; comprehensive in its sympathies and aspirations, it remained rooted in the language and life of provincial Ayrshire farms and smallholdings.

Burns's own poetry complemented rather than distracted from his dual role as the guardian of the folk tradition and a guarantor of liberal anti-monarchical values in the face of the tyrannies of old Europe. 'A Man's a Man for a' That', published in 1795 and set to a Jacobite tune, used a familiar folk world of humble communal solidarity to evoke the possibility of radical change and universal brotherhood. Influenced by traditional song themes, Freemasonry and (probably) the anti-slavery 'Am I Not a Man and a Brother' Wedgwood medallion, it in its turn may well have influenced the revised version of Friedrich Schiller's 'Ode to Joy': *'Alle Menschen werden Brüder'* (All men shall become brothers):

What though on hamely fare we dine,
Wear hoddin grey, an' a that;
Gie fools their silks, and knaves their wine;
A Man's a Man for a' that:
For a' that, and a' that,
Their tinsel show, an' a' that;
The honest man, tho' e'er sae poor,
Is king o' men for a' that ...
... Then let us pray that come it may,
As come it will for a' that,
That Sense and Worth, o'er a' the earth
Shall bear the gree [prize, reward] an' a' that.
For a' that, an' a' that,
It's comin yet for a' that,
That Man to Man the warld o'er
Shall brithers be for a' that.

During the nineteenth century, Burns spread through the British Empire as a symbol of Scottishness and universal humanitarian values. By the centenary of his birth in 1859 there had been almost 20,000 recorded Burns suppers. Burns Clubs formed around the world, and today an estimated 9.5 million attend a Burns supper every year in more than 100 countries. Burns was both a local and a universal poet. The powerful emotional appeal of his work and its emphasis on the importance of sympathy and affection in morals (as championed by Enlightenment thinkers) allowed him to be claimed by radicals and conservatives, communists and freemasons alike. 'A Man's a Man' became not only a song of Romantic brotherhood and German nationalism, but also – in the hands of Frederick Douglass (1817–95) and others – an anthem of the abolitionist movement in the United States.

Burns Overseas

The importance of the 'heart', in many ways the central organ of Scottish Enlightenment morality, is central to Burns' far-reaching global appeal. He was acknowledged in the nineteenth century by nationalist language movements from Norway to the Czech Republic, has influenced leaders of the United Nations and United States, and been quoted by revolutionaries in China (where his songs were used by campaigners against arranged marriage at the beginning of the twentieth century). 'Fusion' Burns suppers are growing in popularity, such as the joint celebration of Burns Night and the Chinese New Year, begun in Vancouver.

By contrast with Burns' rousing if imprecise expressions of sympathy and humanity, Sir Walter Scott's narratives glorified the history of Scotland in detail. While seeming to accept that the country had lost its independence, they also suggested that certain issues remained unresolved. Scott's focus on Scotland was in itself arguably radical in making a case for the country as a real and continuing entity – albeit one imperilled by contemporary trends. Scott also often gave his readers lightly veiled or open references to locations that could be visited, most famously the Trossachs, where *The Lady of the Lake* (1810) delivered a massive and almost instantaneous boost to tourism. Later, the popularity of *Rob Roy* (1817) helped conjure into existence a thriving 'Rob Roy country' – like the Burns country a magnet for international tourists.

Scott's highly coloured vision of the Scottish and medieval pasts appeared to vindicate the Union of Great Britain while at the same time implying that something of what had been lost was worth keeping. Perhaps, many readers inferred, a visit to the vividly evoked settings of his novels might bring them in contact with their fading historical charisma, and reveal something of their secrets. The more acute among them – especially overseas where British patriotism mattered less – were able to discern that some of what had been lost had not just disappeared but been actively and sometimes cruelly suppressed. Some of his books dealt with historical injustice (*The Two Drovers*, *The Highland Widow*, *Redgauntlet*), some with racism (*The Talisman*, *Ivanhoe*, *Guy Mannering*), and most were presented in a Scottish context. Scott offered powerfully comforting stories laced with a hint (more than a hint, in some stories) of disquiet and discomfort.

In France, Scott was seen as an opponent of revolution and a friend of the Royalist cause; in Italy and Hungary, as an avatar of national resistance against imperial power. Everywhere the stamp of his influence was felt in the great age of the novel: in the work of Balzac, Flaubert, Hugo and Stendhal in France; Dickens, Eliot, Hardy and Thackeray in England; James Fenimore Cooper and Mark Twain in North America; Dostoevsky and Tolstoy in the Russian Empire; and Manzoni in Italy.

Painting by John Everett Millais of a scene from Walter Scott's *The Bride of Lammermoor*

In Scott's homeland, inspired by his example, a substantial industry grew up to preserve Scottish history for future generations, while the names of his characters adorned the trains and ships of the steam age. Like Shakespeare, his presence was everywhere in the great age of opera: in the work of Rossini (*La donna del lago*, 1819), Donizetti (*Lucia di Lammermoor*, 1835) and Bizet (*La jolie fille de Perth*, 1867). It was in 1812 that Scott's 'Hail to the Chief' (composed by James Sanderson) was first played 'to honour the end of hostilities and the late George Washington'; since then it has become the theme tune of the US Presidency.

The Romanticisation of Scotland thus took many forms. The presentation of the country at home and abroad as 'the Highlands' tapped into a long tradition of the 'patriot north', according to which northern Scots were the truest. Romantic artists reinforced the association of tartan, pipes and Highland landscapes with the sublimity, beauty and ruin of the Jacobite cause: in Scotland's landscapes, the past was entombed but somehow alive. Lost Scotland was also Scotland revenant. Yet it would not be long before mountains, ruins and tartan – the Highlands – were adopted as a badge of identity by the British Royal Family itself, from the Highland Games to Balmoral.

Tartanised interior of Balmoral in the 1850s, photo by George Washington Wilson

Imperial Scotland

The Victorian era saw the rise of a second British Empire after the loss of the American colonies. Greater in size, this empire was also truly global, with British technological ascendancy providing an infrastructure for commerce as well as power. This was the first modern age of globalisation, in which trade quadrupled – and Scotland was at its forefront.

Scottish networking crossed international and institutional boundaries. Its universities enjoyed a much closer connection with industry than their English counterparts. James Young at what is now the University of Strathclyde opened the first Scottish oil refinery in 1850, while his colleague James Blyth developed the wind turbine. Towering over all was Professor William Thomson (later Lord Kelvin) at the University of Glasgow, whose scientific discoveries helped bring about international telegraphy (in which he was also a major financial investor). Scottish education was more socially open than the English system, and geared to burgh grammar rather than private schools. Though its classless inclusiveness can be overstated, its quality was evident for example in the fact that three French princes attended the Royal High School in Edinburgh.

As during the Enlightenment, Scots showed themselves driven by a passion for ideas, but especially the application of reason to knowledge in service of material improvement. Trade followed the flag. In 1838, the Royal Mail Steam Packet Company was founded by James MacQueen. Brodie McGhie Wilcox and Arthur Anderson's Peninsular and Oriental (P&O, 1840) and the Glasgow-backed Cunard Line (1839) swiftly followed. Together these firms and others like them gave British shipping an 80 per cent share in global trade. Meanwhile, railways lowered the cost of overland transport by over 90 per cent.

The central player in the East Asian opium trade in this era was Jardine Matheson & Co., which operated in Canton from the early 1830s, its fleet carrying a version of the Saltire flag. Founded by William Jardine (1784–1843) and James Matheson (1796–1878), the company persuaded the British government to go to war with China in order to protect its interests: one result was the establishment of a colonial presence in Hong Kong. From 1886 to 1911, a quarter of Clyde-built tonnage was destined for South and East Asia, while in the half-century before the outbreak of the First World War no fewer than seventy-six Scottish investment trusts acquired holdings in tea and rubber.

There were setbacks. In the 1850s, a competitive exam for entry to the Indian Civil Service (ICS) came in, replacing the old system of patronage. This dealt a double blow to Scottish opportunity: as well as threatening Scotland's very active patronage network, the new examination syllabus favoured Oxbridge applicants. Nonetheless, many Scots rose to high office in India. Scots also came to dominate the tea plantations after Francis Mackenzie Gillanders established the first Calcutta tea agency in 1819 with the support of his uncle John Gladstone, a wealthy slave owner and the father of the future prime minister. James Taylor and Sir Thomas Lipton were the most powerful players in the Ceylonese tea market. Indian jute, too, was a major concern for Scottish industry and commerce.

It wasn't all about money. Many Scots engaged deeply with Indian languages, culture and politics. Octavian Hume helped found the country's Congress Party, later led by Gandhi, sowing the seeds of modern Indian nationalism. Later, George Yule (1829–92), former president of the Indian Chamber of Commerce and Sir William Wedderburn, 4th Bart (1838–1918), a member of a Scottish dynasty of civil servants in India, both served as President of Congress.

As they forged the infrastructure of modern business in South and East Asia, Scots abroad were bound together by ties of kinship, place and institutional loyalty. The new common language of Scottish Romanticism helped create an imaginary community throughout the world. St Andrews Day dinners were held in Singapore from 1837, and St Andrews Societies were founded at Jakarta (1838), Shanghai (1865), Hong Kong (1881), Kuala Lumpur (1885), Bangkok (1890) and many other East Asian locations. Burns suppers, too, were major events, with 600 in Shanghai alone in 1902. Haggis was specially imported for these occasions, as at Raffles Hotel in Singapore in 1908. In Shanghai up to 1,500 people might attend the Caledonian Ball, which was the highlight of the city's social calendar.

The power of Scottish networking was widely recognised in the era, with the proverbial 'clannishness' of Scots much commented on. At their peak in the late Victorian period there were more than a thousand Scottish societies throughout Britain and its Empire. These organisations provided help and support for newly arrived or poor Scots, as well as a colourful Scottish Romantic-tinged social life. At the 1879 Waverley Ball at Shanghai, guests dressed as characters from Scott's novels, while at the 1921 St Andrews Ball, clan shields hung on the walls together with Lochaber axes and quotes from Burns and Scott. David Kennedy (1825–86) travelled the world singing Burns and other Scottish songs from 1872 to 1876, with the aim of bringing the songs of Scotland to a global diaspora. Likewise, James Scott Skinner, a Banchory fiddler, toured the US and Canada in 1893, and the Scottish comedians Neil Kenyon and Harry Lauder performed on stages throughout the Empire. The first World Pipe Band Championships were held at Cowal in 1897. Alongside culture, sport helped embed the Scottish brand in the British Empire; in places where Scots were concentrated, English games such as cricket tended to be displaced by more Scottish pursuits. In the absence of embassies, trade missions and other national structures, Scots invested hugely in their social and professional societies. Despite the odd grudging comment, they were more than tolerated by the English.

Scotland thus changed the world, while itself benefiting economically from the technology it did much to pioneer. In 1815 the country's per capita production was 73 per cent of the rest of Great Britain's, with correspondingly lower wages. As the nineteenth century went on, the Scottish economy caught up. Before, capital had mostly been imported into Scotland from the Empire, as the proceeds of slavery in the Caribbean and exploitation in India flowed into the domestic economy. Now, capital was increasingly exported from Scotland. In the United States, 75 per cent of ranch capital – much of it held by women – came from Scotland, amounting to two-thirds of British financial investment in the country. There was also massive Scottish investment in Canada, Australia, India and Ceylon. The Scots' reputation for rigid probity in money matters dates from this era.

From the early nineteenth century, the Indian pattern shawls manufactured in Paisley became a familiar sight in dressmakers' shops and clothing markets around the world. In the years before 1914, Coats of Paisley controlled four-fifths of global threadmaking capacity. Templeton in Glasgow was the largest carpet manufacturer in Great Britain; in Dundee, the city's rapid development as 'Juteopolis' following its earlier linen boom depended on the heavy importation of raw jute, over 140,000 tonnes of which were being landed annually by the 1870s. Indian-style chairs and designs and Chinese-style ceramics – particularly the latter – were mass-produced for export.

Holmwood House, Cathcart (villa by Alexander 'Greek' Thomson)

Architects such as Alexander 'Greek' Thomson (1817–75) injected an eclectic blend of Greek and Egyptian influences into Scotland's domestic architecture. Grand house designs, too, acquired a new flavour with the work of William Burn (1789–1870) and others, whose 'baronial' Gothic style celebrated the country's martial past. Burn's fellow Royal High School pupil, David Bryce (1803–76), remodelled the Duke of Atholl's seat at Blair in this way in 1869.

Although Scotland was now one of Europe's most urbanised countries, emigration remained at Irish or Norwegian levels. Between 1860 and 1914, almost 1 million net migrated out of Scotland, as the Clearances and the opportunities of Empire turbo-charged Scotland's longstanding tradition of sending its people overseas. At first, Australia and New Zealand were the most popular destinations, then the United States and, by the early twentieth century, Canada. Scots dominated Canada's early political development, supplying the Dominion's first and second prime ministers – Sir John Macdonald and Alexander Mackenzie – after Confederation in 1867.

In the United States, Scottish emigrés who made an impact included John Muir (1838–1914), the founder of the National Parks movement; Allan Pinkerton (1819–84), the Gorbals-born cooper, Chartist and head of Union intelligence in the Civil War who is perhaps better known as founder of the Pinkerton's detective agency, and David Dunbar Buick (1854–1929), the carmaker from Arbroath. Scottish societies and newspapers also sprung up on American soil, including the *Scottish Patriot*, *Scotsman* and *Boston Scotsman* and the most successful, the *Scottish-American Journal*, which ran from 1857 to 1919. The American writer Mark Twain characterised the entire American Civil War as a conflict between the followers of Burns (who was one of Lincoln's favourite poets) and those of Scott.

In Africa too, St Andrews and Caledonian Societies were formed at Bulawayo, Gwelo, Nairobi and Zanzibar, with Burns suppers and related musical events popular from Nairobi to Johannesburg. In Salisbury (Harare) in Southern Rhodesia (Zimbabwe), the Caledonian Society offered prizes for Scottish history and poetry, and funded a bursary to pursue the study of the glorious history of Scotland. Indeed the imperial 'scramble for Africa' was partly triggered by a Scot, David Livingstone (1813–73), whose opposition to the Arab-African slave trade went hand-in-hand with his support for British imperial intervention to assure the triumph of what was termed 'commerce and Christianity'. Livingstone's companion Sir John Kirk played a role in the treaty between Great Britain and Zanzibar for the suppression of the slave trade in 1873. Not long after this, students of African descent began to enter Scottish universities, while Black people such as Peter McLagan, who served for twenty-eight years as MP for Bathgate, gained prominence in parts of Scottish society. In 1973, the centenary of Livingstone's death was commemorated by almost three dozen countries in Africa.

Peter McLagan MP (1823–1900), born in Demerara, supporter of women's suffrage, women's education and Irish Home Rule

Continental architecture, art and ideas remained of central importance in Scotland throughout the nineteenth century. In turn, Scottish Romanticism influenced Europe, and inspired the emerging nationalism largely absent in Scotland itself. Hungarian and Italian nationalists such as Lajos Kossuth (1802–94) and Giuseppe Garibaldi (1807–82) were drawn to Scotland and supported the creation of national monuments to Scottish history – notably the Wallace Monument, which opened on the Abbey Craig in Stirling in 1869, a testament to the continuing power of Scottish patriotism and the country's

The Wallace Monument, opened in 1869

awareness of its history. For Garibaldi and his fellow patriot Giuseppe Mazzini (1805–72), Wallace was a hero of Classical stature, a 'High Prophet of Nationality'. Garibaldi even formed a company of Scots in tartan and thistle to fight for him in Italy. In an imperial era that might have been thought more likely to lead to its extinction, Scottish national feeling continued to express itself boldly.

Scots thus enjoyed a distinctive national profile and a soft power that was projected across the globe, underpinned by their country's outstanding achievements and the infrastructure of the British Empire. They were free to pursue their own colonial opportunities even when these brought them into competition with other subjects of the United Kingdom. The only *quid pro quo* was the expectation of loyalty to the Crown and the Union. This paradox was resolved to a degree by the separation of Scotland's patriot history from its dynamic technological present, but from the later nineteenth century, new and distinctive features of Scottish culture were emerging, not all of which were either aligned to English models or subsumed in celebrations of the past.

The world exhibitions, beginning with the 1888 Glasgow International Exhibition, began to foreground Scottish culture. A new generation of historians questioned the age-old idea of a country divided ethnically between Highland Celts and Lowland Saxons. In its wider culture, too, Scotland was increasingly presenting itself in terms of Romantic national unity. The pioneering work of the architect William Burn had already established what was to become known as the Scottish baronial style, presenting a distinctive national perspective in buildings such as Helen's Tower (1848) and Balintore Castle (1859). In Edinburgh, Sir Robert Rowand Anderson's Scottish National Portrait Gallery (1885) offered a vernacular neo-Gothic challenge to the surrounding Georgian New Town, with its Hanoverian names and Unionist identity.

The Scottish National Portrait Gallery

New cultural and historical societies opened, such as the Royal Scottish Geographical Society (1886), the Royal Scottish National Orchestra (1895) and the Scottish Trades Union Congress (1897). In 1889, David McGibbon posited 'The Characteristics of a Scottish National Architecture' at the

Congress of the National Association for the Advancement of Art and its Application to Industry, while Glasgow itself became a major Art Nouveau city. Its leading architect Charles Rennie Mackintosh (1868–1928) and his circle influenced leading European movements such as the Vienna Secession; Mackintosh's wife, the artist Margaret Macdonald (1864–1933), helped shape the work of the artist Gustav Klimt (1862–1918).

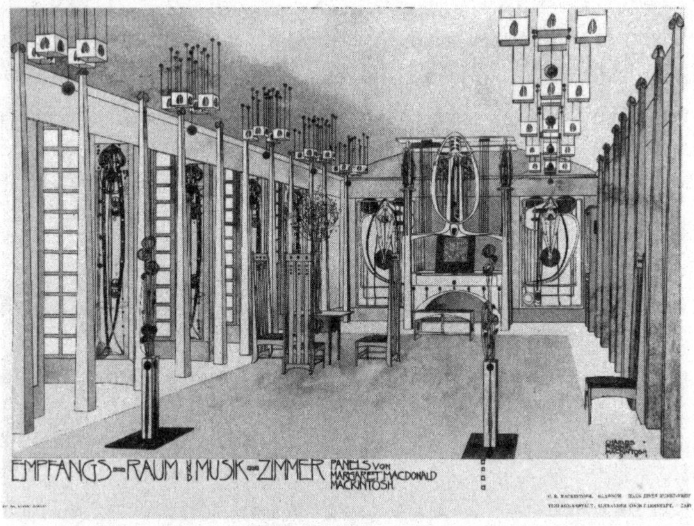

Mackintosh style: design by Charles Rennie Mackintosh for a music room, with panels by Margaret Macdonald

The opportunities for Scots, even those of modest background and means, who gained an education, patronage and the support of an influential circle could be tremendous. The chairman of P&O was the son of a joiner, while the 'Scottish Samurai' Thomas Blake Glover, who did much to found modern Japan, was the son of a coastguard official. Yet many Scots lived in straitened circumstances or were driven by poverty to emigrate. Internally, too, there was substantial migration from the north to eastern and southern Scotland, both for seasonal work such as fruit-picking and for longer-term labour in the cities, typically in heavy industry. Many migrant workers saw their hopes disappointed, living in poor conditions in single rooms in crowded and insanitary tenement flats: there were far more families housed in single rooms in Scotland than in England before the First World War (1914–18), particularly in Glasgow and the west. In 1861, 64 per cent of the country's population lived either in one room or a room and kitchen. Things were better in the smaller towns that depended on agriculture and the professions. The popularity at this time of so-called 'Kailyard' ('Kitchen Garden') literature, which idealised village and small-town life, was largely due to its depiction of a Scotland that no longer existed for most Scots, yet was still reassuringly familiar to many.

Towards the end of the nineteenth century, a view began to form that the problems arising from landlordism in Ireland and Scotland bore deep similarities, encouraging closer ties between the Highland and the Irish Land Leagues. The agricultural disturbances that followed failures in fishing and the potato crop refocused attention on issues of land use in rural Scotland. The Highland Land Law Reform Association (Land League) came into being in 1882–83, with offices in both Edinburgh and London. In 1885, the election of five Crofting MPs – the Crofters' Party was the political wing of the Highland Land League – marked the emergence of a peculiarly Scottish politics for the first time in the modern democratic era, with its five MPs (a sixth followed) all representing a distinctively Scottish political party.

Scottish Romanticism coloured both contemporary politics and interpretations of the past, among them the first modern histories of the Highland Clearances. Celtic society was no longer viewed as savage or disorganised, but as collectivist and ideal. This late Romantic fantasy inspired early leaders of the Scottish Home Rule Association (1886) such as John Stuart Blackie. Other related organisations emerged around this time, including the Liberal Young Scots Society (which had 58 branches by 1914) and the Scottish Patriotic Association (1902), as well as a Scottish branch of the Gaelic League. Such Scottish patriotic and national organisations were often a diluted version of their Irish counterparts. Whereas in Ireland the drift to nationalism drew forth concrete government proposals to try to neutralise it, including Home Rule, Scottish support for equivalent measures was on the whole more tenuous and sentimental.

The power of Scotland's Romantic image abroad, its place at the heart of imperial growth and technological progress, fuelled by vigorous overseas networks of Scottish kith and kin, regiment, school and university, made the long nineteenth century Scotland's era. The First World War was to usher in a long period of slow decline and slower readjustment to Scotland's place in the world – or, increasingly, its lack of one.

CHAPTER 5

MODERN SCOTLAND

Around half of all male Scots under the age of forty-five served in the First World War. Scottish combatants suffered a higher casualty rate than either the British or the British imperial average, though how much higher and why are matters of controversy. Many of the losses were at the hands of Scottish commanders, most notably Douglas, 1st Earl Haig of Bemersyde (1861–1928), who commanded British forces during the offensives at the Somme (1916) and Passchendaele (1917).

Detail from Lorimer's National War Memorial at Edinburgh Castle

The National War Memorial in Edinburgh, designed by Sir Robert Lorimer, commemorates more than 147,000 Scottish casualties from the 1914–18 conflict – a quarter more than

Scotland's share of the British population would seem to warrant. Completed at Edinburgh Castle in 1927, the memorial honours Scotland's dead in unequivocally Scottish national terms.

After the armistice, a huge programme of public building helped rectify the problem of slums in Scottish cities. This was a gesture of solidarity with Prime Minister Lloyd George's 'homes fit for heroes' slogan, invoked south of the border but not acted on to the same extent. Two-thirds of the houses built in Scotland in the inter-war period were public, compared with only a quarter in England and Wales. Many were built to Anglo-British models: it is from around this time that traces of Continental design in Scottish domestic architecture start to wane.

The Logie Estate in Dundee, opened in May 1920, was Scotland's first council housing scheme.

A sense of social mission was felt across Scottish life, not just in public housing. In a country more scarred by the war than the rest of the United Kingdom, a new belief in government intervention, particularly to deliver social welfare, flourished. But there were two edges to the sword. The Munitions Act of 1915, which introduced strict regulation for private factories supplying the military, was an early example of a controlling tendency that quickly eroded the autonomy of Victorian Scottish business. Heavy industries that had been crucial for the war economy found themselves surplus to peacetime requirements, while once-thriving sectors of the Scottish economy, such as textile and coal exports, lost momentum during the war and found it hard to recover.

After the conflict, Scottish business began to dance to a British government tune, and Scottish industry was tethered to a broader national agenda. Enterprise and agility were circumscribed, overseas investment constricted and capital channelled into financing the vast national debt accrued in wartime. This meant that Scotland doubly lost its freedom in both domestic and overseas enterprise. State-directed over-capacity propped up established heavy industries at the expense of their emerging modern successors, a process that persisted all the way up to the closures of the 1980s, when Margaret Thatcher's government abandoned a social mission to support industries such as steel and coal.

The demographic profile of the Scottish population was changing rapidly at this time. By 1911, well over a third of a million people lived in Scotland who had not been born there, mostly immigrants from Ireland. There were also growing numbers of Italians, and a small South and East Asian community sprang up between the wars. Yet Scottish emigration more than counterbalanced such immigration. The net population of the country stagnated as the economy faltered and investment slowed, trends which an increasingly centralised planning cartel of industrial magnates and politicians did little or nothing to reverse. Between 1911 and 1980, almost a quarter of people born in Scotland emigrated. By 1991, Scotland's population was lower than it had been in 1961, and barely 5 per cent higher than it had been in 1931.

Nationalisation and Nationalism

For most of the interwar period, Scotland's economy grew at less than a fifth of the UK average rate. From 1923, when the Scottish railway companies were merged into the British networks, control of the country's major industries gradually moved out of Scotland, a process that was accelerated after the Second World War by the nationalisations of the 1945–51 Labour government. The 1929–32 Depression hit Scotland and its big-ticket industries hard: by 1932 more than half its shipbuilding workers were unemployed. As Scotland's heavy industry faced crisis after crisis at home, the indebtedness of the British Empire after the Great War sapped opportunities for investment overseas. Even so, new domestic institutions were set up in inter-war Scotland, including the National Library of Scotland (1925), the National Trust for Scotland (1931) and the Saltire Society (1936) with its campaigning vision for the preservation and promotion of a distinctive Scottish culture, heritage and history.

Modern Scottish nationalism began to take shape in this impoverished interwar environment, although at first it was the intellectual and cultural pursuit of a very small minority. The Scottish Home Rule Association (SHRA) was re-formed in 1918 to campaign for the devolution of power from Westminster. In 1920, the Scots National League (SNL) was set up by William Gillies (Liam MacGille Losa, 1865–1932), who promoted Gaelic as Scotland's national language, and Ruaraidh Erskine of Mar (1869–1960), founder of *Guth na Bliadhna* (*Voice of the Year*), a magazine which advocated radical constitutional reform as well as the use of Gaelic. While the SHRA was a moderate organisation, the SNL was more uncompromising, closer in its politics to Irish Republicanism. Its mouthpiece, *The Scots Independent* (1926), still survives, but the organisation itself amalgamated with the more moderate SHRA and others in 1928 to form the National Party of Scotland (NPS). A more right-wing and pro-Empire Scottish (Self-Government) Party was founded in 1930, amalgamating with the NPS in 1934 to form the Scottish National Party (SNP). The SNP managed to save its deposit in the odd by-election – and even briefly won a seat at Motherwell in 1945, when not all parties were standing – but it would be several decades before it started to make serious electoral progress.

British policy towards Scotland combined administrative devolution with a gradual alignment of the Scottish economy with British norms. The Scottish National Development Council (1931) and Scottish Economic Committee, as well as the Special Areas Legislation of 1934 and 1937, specifically targeted Scotland. At the same time Scotland was integrated more closely into the bureaucracy of British government. Immediately prior to the war, the Unionist Secretary of State for Scotland Walter Elliot (1888–1958) modernised Scottish local government and supported the creation of a recognisably modern Scottish civil service, nearly all of whose staff were based at St Andrew's House in Edinburgh after it opened in 1936.

A number of soft-power initiatives were launched with Elliot's support. The Empire Exhibition of 1938 in Glasgow was intended to boost the Scottish economy and showcase to the world not only the Empire but also Scotland the brand. The Exhibition – at Bellahouston Park on the city's south side – drew 12.6 million visitors. Elliot's approach to supporting Scottish pride, visibility and employment was an early indicator of what would become a 'regional' strategy. By the Second World War this process of devolution was in full swing, as seen in the establishment of the Scottish Council on Industry and the North of Scotland Hydro Electricity Board in 1943.

Scottish Pavilion, Empire Exhibition (1938)

By this time 'British' identity was beginning to move beyond the hybrid norms of an imperial age – when one could be both British and Canadian, British and South African or indeed British and Scottish – and towards the post-1940 order of 'Britain Stands Alone'. The qualities of an island nation rather than an international empire began to be stressed. British propaganda in the latter part of the war dialled down the imperial voice: in Laurence Olivier's *Henry V* (1944), conceived as a propaganda film, Shakespeare's 'sceptr'd isle' is portrayed as a fundamentally isolated English monarchy, with walk-on parts for the Celtic nations.

The Second World War

England bore the brunt of German bombing during the Second World War, with the horrendous exception of Clydebank, which was almost completely flattened in the March 1941 blitz. Scotland became a training and garrison country

Police and army bomb-disposal officers with a defused German 1000kg '*Luftmine*' (parachute mine) in Glasgow, 18 March 1941

where large numbers of Polish and French expatriate troops were stationed and trained. In total, some 250,000 men of all national backgrounds attended the Commando Combined Training Centre at Inveraray.

Scotland was fortunate in its wartime Secretary of State, Tom Johnston (1881–1965), who was trusted more or less implicitly by Winston Churchill to run the country from 1941. To some degree a supporter of Home Rule, Johnston was strongly in favour of administrative devolution. In 1941 he argued that Scottish MPs should meet in Edinburgh, should have access to a Scottish civil service, and that any Scottish legislation they approved should be rubber-stamped by Westminster. He also suggested forming a Council of State of former Scottish secretaries. This idea had the potential to ease tensions but was rejected in London. Even so, Johnston made a difference, securing a disproportionate share of war contracts for Scotland, helping to set up the Scottish Tourist Board and the Scottish Council for Development and Industry, and making a decisive push for hydroelectric power.

Despite Johnston's vision for a modern Scotland, after the end of the war a new British narrative emerged in which Scotland as a national entity did not feature. The decline of Empire left only one coherent, face-saving version of Britishness: the supreme resistance of 1939–45, begun if not necessarily completed 'alone'. Now, for the first time, the Empire could be a source of British embarrassment rather than pride: the Battle of Britain was a better story than the fall of Singapore.

The 1945 Labour manifesto used 'Britain' and 'British' twenty-six times, with not a single reference to the constituent nations of the United Kingdom. The Conservatives – called Unionists in Scotland until 1965 – spotted this oversight, exploiting it in their 1950 general election manifesto:

> ... until the Socialist Government be removed neither Scotland nor Wales will be able to strike away the fetters of centralisation and be free to develop their own way of life.

The Land and the People

Labour's political programme was built around social class. Its concept of British national solidarity was based on common interests rooted in social justice and equality rather than allowing for individual cultural difference within an overarching imperial identity. There was a marked shift in tone from the Scottish Pavilion of the 1938 Empire Exhibition to the portrayal of 'The Land and the People' of a United Kingdom in the 1951 Festival of Britain. In 1938, the British Empire had been a diverse global project, in which Scotland was a national component of the international identity of Britishness; in 1951, that Britishness was portrayed as the property of a single cohesive island nation with a common culture and language.

Instead of looking outward to Empire, the 1951 Festival was about bringing it all back home. Compared with earlier exhibitions, it was a highly introspective affair. Its vision of British internal diversity was based on immigration into Britain, not on the nationalities already within Britain. Following the arrival of HMT *Empire Windrush* from Jamaica in 1948, with its hundreds of passengers from the Caribbean, multiculturalism became a narrative about the people of Empire returning to the heart of Empire. The red, white and blue star of the Festival replaced both the national flags of the United Kingdom and the multiple flags of Empire. The Festival closed with the singing of 'Jerusalem', with its reference to 'England's green and pleasant land'.

There was a tension between this vision of Great Britain as a single unified state rather than a multinational one, and ongoing administrative devolution to Scotland. Ironically, both contributed to undermining the long-standing autonomy of Scottish institutions. The nationalisations of 1945–51 effectively moved control of major heavy Scottish industries to London. New developments such as the 1948 Clyde Valley electricity supply plan were based on norms from south of the border – if the promises of 'Supply to Remotest Parts' and 'standard size and voltage' made by the nationalised power industry were welcome to many Scots, they also imposed a unwanted British homogeneity on the junior national partner.

Public spending and central planning began to weaken local enterprise and innovation in many parts of Scotland. While new agencies and enterprises might be called 'Scottish' and operate separately from their UK counterparts, their policies pursued a central government agenda. When factories were set up, as in West Lothian or Linwood in response to an 'Inquiry into the Scottish Economy', head offices and other key parts of the business typically stayed south of the border. Operations on the ground often suffered as a result. Linwood's car plant was built to compensate for Scotland's loss of heavy industry, but its iconic model, the Hillman Imp, was a classic 'branch line' product, half-baked, neglected and soon outclassed.

Launched in 1963, the Hillman Imp was marketed as a fun and affordable alternative to the Mini. Less fun was the tendency of its rear engine to overheat.

A new rhetoric of Britain as a unitary nation state accompanied these changes. In the Empire's heyday, calling oneself 'Scottish and British' made sense; on a single island, less so. Second World War planning documents described Scotland for the first time as a 'region' of the United Kingdom. The Beveridge Report of 1942, which limned out the foundations of the modern welfare state, pushed UK-wide solutions without taking into account Scottish national circumstances. In the past, such neglect or inattention had mostly been sporadic and unintended. Now it was part and parcel of a concerted programme of central planning and policy coming out of London.

The leading Scottish nationalist John MacCormick was at the forefront of resistance to these changes, notably through the 1949–52 Covenant movement, which gathered 1.7 million signatures in support of Scottish Home Rule. Clearly, many were dissatisfied with the political settlement in Scotland. In 1950, in a stunt which attracted much media publicity, a group led by Ian Hamilton (1925–2022), later a well-known lawyer and nationalist, removed the Stone of Destiny – on which Scottish kings were traditionally crowned – from Westminster to Scotland. This was only the most prominent in a series of tokenistic gestures of resistance that also included assaults on an Edinburgh postbox bearing the legend 'E II R' – Elizabeth being not the second but the first queen of that name in Scotland. New postboxes henceforth bore the simple legend 'E R'. In 1953 MacCormick even took to the courts to challenge Elizabeth's right to style herself 'II' in Scotland. He lost the cause on most counts, but the judge, Lord Cooper the Lord President, gave a separate non-binding opinion that 'the principle of unlimited sovereignty of Parliament is a distinctively English principle and has no counterpart in Scottish constitutional law' – an affirmation of the principle of Scottish popular sovereignty. Notably, Lord Cooper had been a Unionist MP from 1935 to 1941, though he adhered to the strongly patriotic Scottish Unionism that appealed to a broad swathe of the Scottish electorate at this time.

Although a number of new national organisations and institutions such as Scottish Television (STV, 1955) and Scottish

Opera (1962) were founded under the 1951–64 Conservative governments, the overall current continued to flow strongly towards centralisation. Like Linwood car plant, attempts to revive the Scottish economy such as the Fort William pulp and paper mill (1964) and the Invergordon aluminium smelter (1968) all ultimately foundered. Moving just one element in a centralised business simply raised costs and lowered connectivity and efficiency. With no stake in leadership and innovation, such branches were always likely to wither in the long term. Indeed, Scotland itself – in a previous century home to global corporations – was becoming an impoverished branch line of the British economy.

Beeching Cuts: the Waverley Route through the Borders was closed in 1969. Here a train approaches the village of Riccarton Junction.

The Beeching railway cuts of the 1960s underlined the whole situation. The scythe fell disproportionately on Scotland, which suffered the closure of the entire Borders railway. By 1961, Scotland's GDP per capita had sunk to 86 per cent of the UK average. Levels of emigration rose even further: from 1951 to 1981, the outflow of people exceeded any natural increase in population. Nor was this compensated for by newcomers from the Commonwealth. By the 1970s, it was clear that little of the immigration into the UK as a whole was going into Scotland, where population levels continued to flatline.

Scotland's ability to represent itself to its own people was also becoming an issue. Since the Victorian period, Scottish newspapers had played an important part in protecting and promoting regional, national and even linguistic identity. They continued to dominate the Scottish print market, but broadcasting media were on the rise and they took a very different tack. The London-based British Broadcasting Corporation (BBC) was an avatar of a new centralist approach in the 1920s and 1930s; this became entrenched during the Second World War. The BBC spent far less of its licence fee revenue on the regions – and nations – outside London. Scotland was no exception. Moreover, the BBC depiction of Scotland dwelt on stereotypes, while news and current affairs focussed heavily on 'national' (i.e. London) as opposed to regional events. There was no place for a 'four nations' agenda, and to some extent this situation endures. Radio Scotland was not founded until 1978; in the meantime it was left to the independent companies, STV and Grampian in particular, to articulate a sense of Scottishness.

The dissolution of the British Empire had a further profound effect on Scotland. The Empire had long provided opportunities for Scots abroad. Three in every five Scottish school history textbooks discussed the Empire, and almost a quarter of history questions for the Scottish Leaving Certificate addressed it in one way or another. By 1960, the the end was nigh: almost twenty colonies would become independent in the next four years. The global projection, power and significance of Great Britain was drawing to an close, and many of the opportunities Scots had won with the Union of 1707 were now dying with it. The growing global dominance of American businesses and brands, combined with an emphasis on British policy and British institutions at home, further undermined Scotland's social and cultural autonomy.

The slow decline of the influence of the Kirk on domestic social mores reinforced this process, with ongoing secularisation accompanying other major changes in Scottish society. In 1958, Christmas became a public holiday in Scotland (though it remained a normal working day in many parts of the country into the 1960s). Boxing Day followed in 1973. Lingering Presbyterian distrust of any festival with 'Mass' in the title eroded as Scotland became more secular.

MINERS TOOK A DAY OFF

Although Christmas Day is not recognised as a holiday in the Scottish coalfields, 35 per cent of the 2300 miners in the seven collieries in the Shotts district were absentees on Wednesday.

The cost was nearly 600 tons of coal.

The *Midlothian Advertiser* notes the cost of Christmas on 27 December 1946

With the 1707 Union, Scotland lost its already limited sovereignty as an international political actor. In exchange, it gained access to huge territories where it could exercise soft power and make money, and many of its institutions remained autonomous. This arrangement no longer held. A 1954 Royal

Commission made the case for administrative devolution on a grand scale, reporting as follows:

> The Commission proposed ... that the responsibilities of the Minister of Transport and Civil Aviation in Scotland for roads, piers and ferries, the responsibility of the Lord Chancellor for the appointment of justices of the peace, and the responsibilities of the Minister of Agriculture and Fisheries for animal health, should all be transferred to the Secretary of State for Scotland ... The Commission made a number of recommendations of an administrative character, designed inter alia to increase the amount of Scottish business which the United Kingdom and Great Britain Departments can settle in Scotland. The Government is in full accord with the objectives of the Commission and hopes to be able to give effect to most of their detailed recommendations.

However, the relative decline in Scotland's economy and its institutions continued.

By the 1960s, almost all of the 200 Scottish trade unions operating in 1900 had disappeared, and the country's stock exchanges were following them into oblivion. In 1962, the appearance in schools of the 'O' grade, a transparently tartanised O level that partially replaced the old Leaving Certificate, launched a process of Anglicisation in Scottish school education that was only halted – though not reversed – by strong professional resistance in the ensuing decades. In 1962, the University of Edinburgh became the first university in Scotland to join a UK-wide central clearing system; by 1985 all Scotland's universities had followed suit.

Scottish education was becoming more British, and many of its distinct practices were being lost. Yet it was those very practices that had long made Scottish education so successful. Now it became more homogeneous, more intellectually egalitarian and more like education elsewhere in the UK (though retaining its own secondary examination structure and with less specialism in higher education and the final years of school).

One of the ironies of modern, post-devolution Scotland is that, as the English education system has evolved to provide an ever greater range of opportunities, successive Scottish administrations of all stripes have continued to defend an ossified system based on a British Labour comprehensive-school agenda that has remained fundamentally unchanged since the 1960s. One-size-fits-all is not how Scottish education gained its reputation.

Scotland's heavy industries enjoyed a brief window of success in the years after the Second World War, when the world was rebuilding its damaged and disrupted economies. The Clyde shipyards launched one-third of global tonnage in 1950. By 1960, it was 5 per cent. Industries were nationalised and subsidised, and began to perform a social rather than an economic mission, keeping people in employment in areas that would be most impacted by the closure of plants, mines or other works. Between 1955 and 1965, the Scottish deficit within the National Coal Board was £136 million, to take just one example.

At the same time, control of private industry and finance was fast slipping out of Scottish hands, damaging the Unionists with their stress on local control within the United Kingdom. Building societies, hitherto marginal in Scotland, began to push banks out of the deposit market, while Scotland's historical strengths in life and general assurance began a slow decline.

The unemployment, child poverty, poor health and other social problems associated with the relentless decline of labour-intensive heavy industry were particularly severe in west-central Scotland with its high population density. Central planning displaced dynamic individual enterprise. Nationalisation and the globalisation of capital drew power to the centre. Regional policies sometimes used taxpayers' money to repatriate low-paid (i.e. relatively cheap) manufacturing and assembly jobs, but by the 1990s, Scotland had less than half of the UK private sector's research and development spend per capita.

These changes were reflected in Scottish politics. At the 1955 general election, the Unionists and their allies won thirty-six of Scotland's seventy-one seats, and (though they lost seats) they returned about half of the popular vote four years later. In 1965, the Unionists merged with the Conservative Party of England and Wales to form the Conservative and Unionist party. In the 1966 election the new organisation won just twenty seats, and would never be as successful as its predecessor.

It was around this time that the longstanding role of the Unionist party as the patriotic defender of Scotland's history, culture and institutions began to weaken – after all, they were no longer even a Scottish party following their amalgamation with the Conservatives. This left a vacancy for another party that could defend the old patriot Unionist ground. The SNP stepped in, giving Scots an opportunity to demonstrate their dissatisfaction and difference. On 2 November 1967, the Glasgow solicitor Winnie Ewing (1929–2023) won the Hamilton by-election with a colossal swing of 38 per cent, one of the largest of all time. Ewing had always had an ear for the arresting phrase, and she campaigned to 'Put Scotland Back on the Map'. Her acceptance speech included the catchy sentence 'Stop the world, Scotland wants to get on' – later the title of her autobiography. Although Ewing lost Hamilton in the next general election, she had a career spanning thirty years in various parliaments, and her party never ceased thereafter to be a major force.

Winnie Ewing: 'Stop the World, Scotland Wants to Get On'

The late 1960s were fertile ground for a political realignment, being critical for both Scotland and Great Britain. The Empire was now unequivocally at an end, and it was clear that the UK would have to form a new identity – or identities – to replace it. In August 1969, the Unionist government of Northern Ireland urgently requested the deployment of British troops to assert the authority of the Crown in the province: the first conflict of the Empire was to be one of the last. In the 1970s as in the 1650s, the plantation of Ulster had to be defended by troops from the neighbouring island, with more than 20,000 deployed at the peak of the Troubles. The 1966–70 Labour government had been in power for only four years, but the changes those years had brought would last much longer.

Although the performance of the SNP in the 1970 general election fell short of the political threat that the party seemed to carry after Hamilton, the British government continued to pay attention to the issue of Scottish governance. A Royal Commission on the Constitution was set up in 1969, and four years later finally recommended a Scottish Assembly – albeit one with unspecified powers (the Commission's members having been unable to agree on this point). By now an additional complicating factor was the European Economic Community (EEC, later the EU), which the UK had joined on 1 January 1973 and later endorsed in a 1975 referendum. Some members of the Royal Commission took the view that powers which would eventually migrate to Brussels should not be devolved in the interim.

The victory of the SNP's Margo MacDonald in the Govan by-election in November 1973, eight days after the Royal Commission had reported, lent a sense of electoral urgency to the Scottish constitutional question. This was only deepened by the general election in the autumn of the following year, in which the SNP won eleven seats but took over 30 per cent of the vote, coming second in thirty-six constituencies. The eventual result was the Scotland Bill of 1977 – inconsistent, unclear on the crucial subject of precisely which powers were devolved, and granting quasi-viceregal powers to the Secretary of State. A popular referendum was held on the Bill, with a stipulation that 40 per cent of the electoral roll had to vote in favour, and with an opt-out for Orkney and Shetland if they voted against.

The referendum, held on 1 March 1979, saw a narrow majority of voters in favour (52 to 48 per cent), but with overall turnout below 65 per cent, the 40 per cent hurdle was not reached. The immediate outcome was a further rapid decline in support for the SNP.

However, despite the appearance of renewed engagement in

British politics, in the longer term Scotland became more and more detached from the south. Support for outright independence, as low as 14 per cent in 1979, more than doubled in the ensuing decade and continued to grow. Although the Conservative governments of 1979–97 watered down their policies in Scotland (with the signal exception of the poll tax, which they introduced in 1988, a year earlier in Scotland than elsewhere in the UK, gifting the SNP an opportunity they duly took advantage of), they were still widely resented as illegitimate.

Scottish anti-poll tax protesters at Westminster in February 1989

Scotland's electoral behaviour was diverging more and more from England's. At first it was the Labour Party who benefitted: the 1979 election saw a small swing to Labour in Scotland, in stark contrast to the rest of Great Britain. In the 1980s the party was helped by an ill-advised attempt to outflank it from the left by the Nationalists. But as independence began to replace devolution as a priority for many Scots, voters turned to the SNP.

Socially and culturally, Scotland was still a very different place from England. Middle-class identity was unpopular, seen as pretentious and even non-national, particularly in the west. However, New Towns such as Cumbernauld and East Kilbride drew large numbers from inner-city Glasgow – proportionally more than their south-eastern English counterparts such as Hatfield and Basildon attracted from London. The aspirational but solidly lower-middle-class experience of such towns and their hesitant modernity is brilliantly captured in the 1981 film *Gregory's Girl*, which portrays a new generation of Scots moving away from the cramped inner cities into the brave new worlds of secularism and gender equality.

In 1981, on the eve of the Conservative government's sell-off of council homes, more than half of Scots lived in public housing, compared with only 32 per cent elsewhere in the United Kingdom. Three quarters of all Scottish houses built from 1950 to 1980 were in this category – even higher than in the inter-war era. Scots today still differ sharply from other British people in their attitudes to social equality. The general rise in prosperity between 1980 and 2000 (central heating up from 53 to 93 per cent of homes, freezers from 41 to 96 per cent) did not swing voters noticeably to the right, unlike in England where the same developments made life more difficult for the left and Labour.

Despite the weakness of nationalist political parties in Scotland in this period, there was a discernible move towards stronger expressions of cultural nationalism. Alasdair Gray's *Lanark* (1981), Iain Banks's *The Wasp Factory* (1984), James Kelman's *The Busconductor Hines* (1984), Liz Lochhead's *Mary Queen of Scots Got Her Head Chopped Off* (1987) and Irvine Welsh's *Trainspotting* (1993) were among the literary works that interrogated Scotland's social and cultural malaise.

Television and cinema joined the party, turning the spotlight on the bleakly native in series such as *Rab C. Nesbitt* (1988–99, 2008–14), *Tutti Frutti* (1987), *Taggart* (1983–2010) and the film adaptation of *Trainspotting* (1996). Folk music revived, most famously with the Corries (whose nostalgic 'Flower of Scotland', written in 1966, attained the status of a sporting national anthem), but also with a host of other Scottish bands. Gaelic rock grew in popularity from the 1970s on, Runrig being one of the best-known examples. By the end of the 1980s there was clearly an appetite for national depictions of Scottishness, even if the version of the nation they portrayed was partial and incomplete.

The dominance of the Conservative Party in UK elections and its perceived intransigence towards Scotland between 1979 and 1997 helped revive civic interest in devolution. After the 1987 general election, when the Conservatives in Scotland were reduced to just ten seats, the Claim of Right (1988) was drafted by the Campaign for a Scottish Assembly, with broad support across the opposition parties. This declaration mimicked the language of the Scottish Parliament of three centuries earlier in claiming sovereignty for the Scottish people. A cross-party Constitutional Convention was set up the following year, and began devising a workable system of Scottish governance.

The SNP declined to participate, afraid of having to play cheerleader to whatever a Labour-dominated Convention might determine, and – as with devolution in 1979 – wary of being blamed for a project they did not originate. Instead they aligned themselves more closely with the EEC through an 'Independence in Europe' strategy, and were rewarded in 1994 with 34 per cent of the vote in the European elections, despite a wider British controversy over European political and economic integration. In that year, a poll showed that support for a joint Scottish and European identity 'to some degree' was the identified preference of 64 per cent of SNP voters.

In their 1997 general election manifesto, Tony Blair's Labour party pledged a referendum on Scottish devolution. The pledge was honoured, but once in power a resurgent Labour tended to row back on the language of Scottish sovereignty and the Scottish people's right to determine their own destiny in favour of the customary Westminster emphasis on its own sovereignty.

The referendum asked two questions: should there be a Scottish Parliament; and should it have tax-varying powers? The answer to the first was a resounding 'Yes' (74 to 26 in favour, with a positive result for every area in Scotland), with a solid 63 per sent in favour of tax-varying powers (the only 'Nos' coming from Galloway and Orkney).

The Secretary of State for Scotland, Donald Dewar (1937–2000), who became Scotland's first First Minister in 1999, was a man of shrewdness and ability who also understood constitutional precedent. In 1998, his Scotland Act was introduced. Based on Gladstone's ideas on Irish Home Rule in the late nineteenth century, it stipulated the powers to be reserved to Westminster instead of those that would be devolved to Edinburgh, and was thus much cleaner than the 1970s legislation. A First Minister would lead a Scottish Executive in the Parliament – the downgrade to 'Executive' from 'Government' lingered from the 1970s, though this was changed in practice by the SNP and confirmed in law by Westminster in 2012.

Foreign affairs, defence, macroeconomic policy, social security and the constitution headed the list of powers that were reserved to the Westminster government. Sceptics of devolution in the Labour party secured the addition of broadcasting, drugs, firearms and equal opportunities, as well as abortion and related issues, and monopolies and mergers. The new arrangement gave some scope for intergovernmental cooperation within the United Kingdom, but this was always stronger in theory than in practice.

Elections to the new Parliament in May 1999 resulted in a 'progressive' Labour–Liberal Democrat coalition, the ideal of Tony Blair's new politics. The SNP won thirty-five seats on 28 per cent of the overall vote, becoming the official opposition. From the beginning, long before the SNP came to power in 2007, the Scottish Parliament saw itself not as a sub-state regional government, but as a 'reconvened' national parliament, as Winnie Ewing, with her gift for historic quotation, described it during its first session in 1999:

> The Scottish Parliament, adjourned on the twenty-fifth day of March in the year 1707, is hereby reconvened.

The institution's view of itself seemed to be shared by the electorate. In a major poll that same year, 46 per cent of Scots thought that their parliament would be the most important element in Scotland's governance in twenty years' time, with 31 per cent opting for the European Union and only 8 per cent for Westminster. This was a far cry from the pecking order in the minds of the Blair government and its successors.

Dewar's speech at the Scottish Parliament's official opening, echoing that of the Irish nationalist leader Charles Stewart Parnell at Cork in 1885, spoke of the country as being on a journey. The fact that Dewar had pressed at Westminster for a devolutionary model very similar to Gladstone's Irish one lent constitutional weight to the implied comparison. Most importantly, it was a statement of Scottish nationality, a 'we' that transcended the constitutional arrangements of sub-state government.

Scottish Parliament Building, Holyrood, Edinburgh

Under the SNP from 2007, the underlying belief that the devolved government was a restoration of Scotland's national parliament became explicit. As more powers devolved to Scotland over the following years, the message was that the Scottish nation was in a governing partnership with England. The Calman Commission on Scottish Devolution went so far as to state in 2009 that the United Kingdom had never been a unitary state, and that Westminster sovereignty was a mere 'convention'. On the other side, the idea that any form of devolution dangerously compromised the power of Westminster would rear its head again in the Brexit referendum of 2016. But first came another vote, this time on Scottish independence.

In their first term in office, the SNP under Alex Salmond had started a 'National Conversation' as a prelude to a further referendum on the creation of a separate Scottish state. In 2011, the SNP won an overall majority in a Scottish general election with 45 per cent of the vote, and proceeded to legislate for such a referendum. This was a remarkable political sea-change. The British government – confident of a big victory which would settle the issue – consented to the referendum in 2012.

The campaign that followed lasted almost two years and reached into every corner of Scottish society. The Yes campaign was everywhere; the Better Together (No) campaign, led by Alistair Darling, the former Labour Chancellor, had a lower profile on the streets, if not in the media. It focused on the dangers and risks of independence, particularly with regard to currency, the economy, pensions, EU membership and oil revenues.

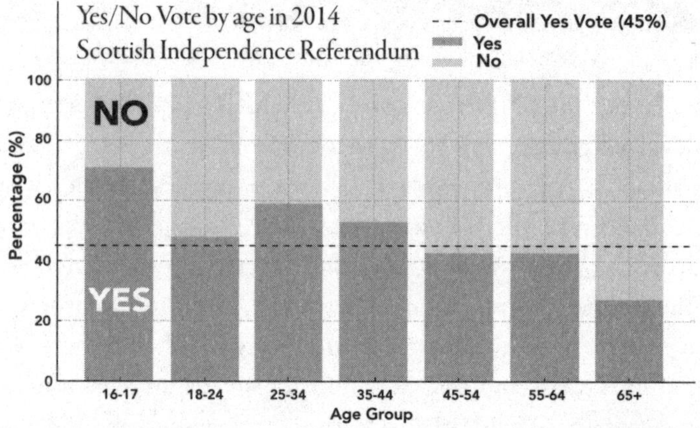

The independence referendum saw an 85 per cent turnout across Scotland – almost a full turnout, given the vagaries and duplications of the electoral register. The result was far closer than most had expected. In the end, 45 per cent voted Yes to complete sovereign status and the creation of an independent Scottish state under the British Crown. Three of Scotland's thirty-two local authorities registered a Yes vote, including the cities of Glasgow and Dundee. A majority of Scots-born voters opted Yes, as did most of those under fifty-five, irrespective of origin; and there appears to have been a majority Yes vote from the Scots Asian community. And yet the overall answer was No. In the wake of this victory, the British Prime Minister David Cameron rather gracelessly proclaimed that in future there would be 'English votes for English laws' at Westminster from which Scots MPs would be excluded.

Two years later, Scotland demonstrated, not for the first time, how different a country it was from England. In the June 2016 referendum on leaving the European Union, all thirty-two of Scotland's local authority areas voted to remain in the EU. The SNP – which had won fifty-six of the fifty-nine Scottish seats at the 2015 UK general election – was solidly pro-EU as a party, but its voters were more divided. Though many SNP supporters voted Leave (35–40 per cent), they were typically also in favour membership of the European Free Trade Association or the European Economic Area, rather than the swashbuckling Singapore-upon-Thames vision of the ardent English Brexiteer leadership. The issues of absolute sovereignty or immigration ('Take Back Control') that had played starring roles in the Leave campaign had little traction in Scotland.

Reality Bites: Brexit and Cakeism

After initial gains for the Tories in 2017, once faced with an extreme version of Brexit, Scottish voters began to drift back towards the SNP. In the final European election in which the UK participated, in 2019, the Brexit Party topped the poll throughout England and Wales, barring London. In Scotland, the SNP won in every local authority area.

Twenty-five per cent of those who voted Labour in Scotland in the UK general election of 2019 reported that

Brexit had pushed them towards Scottish independence. Support for independence and for the SNP rose to over 50 per cent in the final year before the 2021 Scottish elections. Despite the challenge of a new nationalist party, Alba, led by former First Minister Alex Salmond, Nicola Sturgeon's SNP won comfortably, being only one seat off an overall majority. For 49 per cent of voters, the independence question was the most important issue in the run-up to the vote, ahead of education (28 per cent) and health (27 per cent). Getting the British government to agree to hold a second referendum was quite another matter.

As the SNP's fourth term in office progressed, internecine disagreements, controversial legislation and rumours of corruption and scandal damaged the government in Scotland. Support for independence remained strong, but the Nationalists' apparent inability to make it happen seriously eroded their support. To be fair, given the post-Brexit emphasis on British unity and the lack of a clear majority for a Scottish state, the Nationalists were in a very difficult position – but they had also failed to manage expectations. More importantly, they had failed to build a cultural and political consensus for the creation of a new state across Scottish society. Instead, in the eyes of some veteran nationalists, they were seen as doing things *to* Scotland rather than *with* Scotland – for example, by going into coalition with the Greens, or by championing socially divisive legislation. All this rendered the SNP vulnerable to well-timed interference from the British government and the more moderate fiscal and social policies of a resurgent Labour Party. Outflanking Labour on the left had not worked when the SNP were a minority party; there was no sign that it would be any more successful when the Nationalists were in government.

Since 2014, support for independence has grown only

marginally, despite the potential harm caused by Brexit to the Scottish economy. At first the Nationalist government under Nicola Sturgeon (First Minister, 2014–23) set a very reasonable target of 60 per cent support for independence before pressing for another referendum. But it soon buckled to the demands of newer party members with a more utopian outlook. Since 2017, the SNP has been pushing for a fresh referendum with no means of compelling the UK government to concede it – or, importantly, the support needed to be certain of winning it. As a result, they have appeared weak.

Brexit's consequences are profound and far-reaching, but at the electoral level its effect has been more marginal. The British government continues to encroach on the powers of the Scottish Parliament – for example through the Internal Market Act of 2020 – without suffering any ill effects at the ballot box, encouraging Labour to move onto the Tories' ground.

A core problem for the Scottish independence cause is that the independence people seek often remains very British in nature, as polls make clear. Many Scots desire not so much a separate state as a rejigged arrangement in which they keep the parts of the British system they like (i.e. health, welfare and benefits) and jettison others they like less. Supporters of the Union are able to exploit this conditional support for quasi-independence, confident that their stress on the supposed economic risks of voting Yes will strike home. At the same time, voters with a 'British preference' are unswayed when the SNP denigrates British institutions like the NHS, for whose failings within Scotland they are as likely to blame the Nationalists as Westminster.

All this could play into the hands of Labour. It is noteworthy that the British institutions and policy issues most closely associated with the Tories – the Crown and immigration –

have much less consent in Scotland than those most closely associated with Labour, such as the welfare system. Beneath many SNP voters, a British Labour voter still lies in wait – and until this changes, pressure for independence will stay vulnerable and provisional. The SNP has for a long time convinced many Scots that it is the best choice to manage the Labour state, but a Labour state it remains.

Many Scots who apparently support the creation of a new state are more interested in an idealised version of Britain than somewhere genuinely different. Cakeism – the belief that one can have one's political and economic cake and eat it too – is not the sole province of the Brexiteer. For large numbers of its supporters, independence is not a means of building a new Scotland replete with both risks and opportunities, but a simple, catch-all solution to the problems they see in contemporary society. Tough decisions about structural reform, cultural renewal and economic growth all lie at the margins of discussions about independence, not at the centre. Although support for independence remains high, structural discontents with the functioning of the UK state and political system have made the Reform Party in Scotland more popular than any previous right-wing Unionist party. Support remains weaker than south of the border, but a breakthrough result in future Scottish parliamentary elections looks more than likely.

Devolution has been a success. In 2019, Scotland's GDP stood at £180.4bn, equivalent to £33,200 per capita for a population of 5.4 million. Despite low levels of private-sector research and development spending, Scotland has done relatively well in boosting the efficiency of its workers and businesses. Scottish productivity, around 10 per cent lower than the UK average in 2008, was within 1 per cent of that average ten years later, and continues to rise more than twice as quickly. Elsewhere, the Scottish government's close links with universities, awareness of their economic impact, excellence in research and high concentration of spin-out companies are a positive contrast to the suspicion with which many policymakers south of the border view higher education. Exports of goods are also growing strongly.

Energy, financial services, engineering, construction and the cultural and creative industries are today Scotland's largest economic sectors. Though North Sea oil and gas still contribute a sizeable chunk of GDP, renewables accounted for 90 per cent of Scotland's gross electricity production in 2019, up from 59 per cent four years earlier. A target of 100 per cent had been set for 2020 and the final number was only just shy of this – an impressive feat given the hugely ambitious goals set by Alex Salmond's administration a decade earlier. Scotland's leading role in combating climate change was recognised as early as 2009, at the COP15 summit in Copenhagen.

There are problems, of course. Scotland's higher public spending gives it a larger deficit than the rest of the UK, while its small and medium-sized enterprises export less. On paper, Scots today are roughly as well off as the English – but, like England, the country has major internal inequalities, so GDP per capita figures are not the whole story. Fewer than five hundred people own half of Scotland's private rural land, and average pay in different locations can vary by up to 30 per cent. Some cities have grown strongly in recent decades, but rural areas and urban hinterlands often lack money and opportunity.

Global Threads in the Tartan

In 2015, 40 per cent of Scots thought new arrivals from abroad improved the country. Until recently, polls showed a general uptick in consent for immigration to Scotland, which its governments have supported since Jack McConnell's Labour-led administration of 2001–7. The Scots are far less likely than the English to worry about a 'clash of civilisations' between Islam and the West.

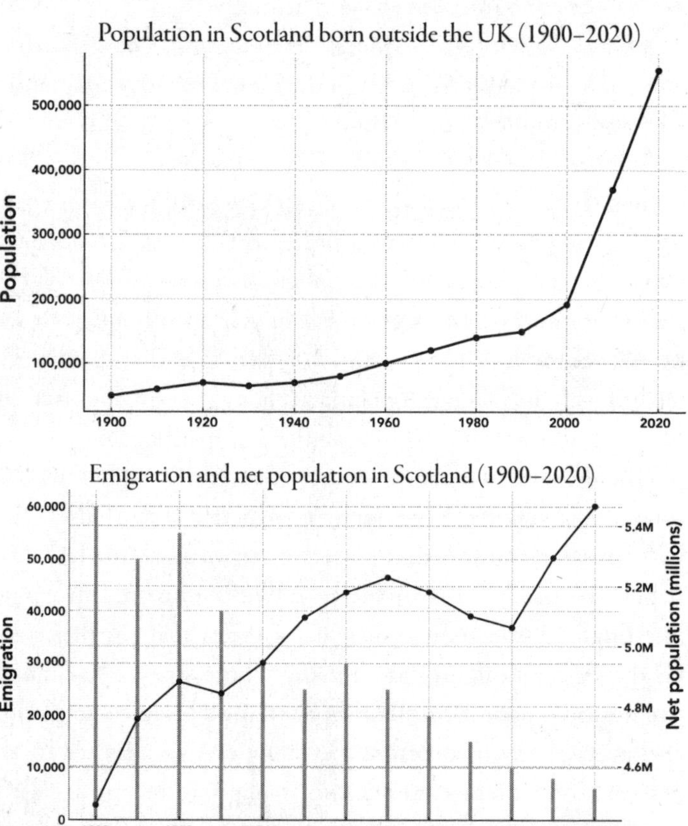

Scottish society has diversified considerably since the 1960s and 70s. By 2011 there were 82,000 Scots of South Asian origin and almost 34,000 ethnic Chinese born in Scotland. Scottish Muslims (mostly South Asian) tend to be more patriotic than their coreligionists south of the border. In Scotland, the community of Pakistani origin is far more likely to identify as Scots (31 per cent) or mixed (Pakistani/British/Scottish = 56 per cent) than Pakistani alone (13 per cent), and is at least as likely to support Scottish independence as other members of the general population. Today's Scotland is more and more sceptical of British institutions – in 2021 fewer than half of all Scots thought the BBC's news and current affairs coverage did a good job at representing their lives – but also more at ease and confident in itself.

Tartan, once the cloth of dress balls and nationalist eccentrics, has been on a half-century roll since it was revived by popular musicians such as Slade, Rod Stewart and Andy Cameron, with his 'Ally's Tartan Army' World Cup song of 1978. Vivienne Westwood has helped repurpose it into a symbol of punk rebellion. By the later 1980s, tartan was becoming fashionable again – a collective badge of identity that to start with was most obvious at weddings. New Scots adopted what was once seen as a marker of bloodline inheritance, and Sikh, Chinese, Pakistani and Polish tartans appeared. Tartan has continued to be a powerful fashion signifier into the twenty-first century.

Vivienne Westwood tartan

Gaelic writing and the Gaelic language have seen a resurgence in Scottish culture since the 1960s. The Historical Dictionary of Scots Gaelic was founded in 1966 and the Gaelic Books Council three years later. From the early 1970s, Sabhal Mòr Ostaig in Skye pioneered higher education in Gaelic, and the following decade Comunn na Gàidhlig (1984) was set up to promote the use of Gaelic among younger people, including in schools. The Gaelic Language Act (2005) established Bòrd na Gàidhlig as an executive public body of the Scottish government, boosting the language's official status. From 1989, Gaelic broadcasting received an injection of dedicated funding, backed by a legal obligation under the 1991 Broadcasting Act. BBC Alba was launched in 2008 after a £12m investment from the Scottish government. By 2011 it was reaching an average audience of 530,000, and helping make the Gaelic language an accepted and valued part of the cultural landscape.

In more recent years, a national Gaelic language plan has placed bilingual obligations on public bodies as well as educators. In 2021, there were at least 137 nurseries and primary or secondary schools offering classes of one sort or another in Gaelic. The language also appeals to the Scottish diaspora overseas, and is now taught in Canada, Germany, Sweden and the United States among other countries. Online language learning apps such as Duolingo were feeding a community of some 1.5 million Gaelic learners by late 2022, one-third of them from the United States. Meanwhile the Scots language – competence in which was the subject of a question for the first time in the 2011 census – also has its champions online as well as in print. The first edition of the *Scottish National Dictionary* appeared in 1976, while W.L. Lorimer's *New Testament in Scots* (1983) was a further sign of the slow but steady growth of a Scots publishing industry. The study of at least some Scottish literature in schools is now compulsory at Higher level (the equivalent of sixth form). In 2021, the search engine Firefox introduced a Scots-language browser, which within two years had attracted over 130,000 users.

Famously, there are dozens of Aberdeens, Edinburghs, Hamiltons and other towns and cities throughout the world, all named after a Scottish original. The number of Americans reporting Scottish ancestry is roughly the same as the population of Scotland itself. For many years, North America has been the most energetic arena for Scottish diasporic activity. The Association of Scottish Games and Festivals was founded in 1981, as was the Scottish American Military Society. Pipe bands and especially Highland Games continue to nourish a performative Scottishness througout the continent, with more than 200 active clan societies and 125 pipe bands reported in the last decade of the twentieth century. By 2000 there were 205 Highland Games in the United States.

It was in Nova Scotia in 1987 that 6 April, the date of the Declaration of Arbroath, was first ratified as Tartan Day, intended to celebrate Scottish ancestry and Scotland's place in North American culture. In 1998, US Senate Resolution 155, formally entered Tartan Day into the calendar. One result has been an annual themed Tartan Week in New York. Not everyone has been enamoured in Scotland itself, where many educated types are somewhat allergic to what they see as nostalgic flummery (despite the growing domestic popularity of all things tartan).

This discomfort – an uneasy strain that runs through modern Scottish culture – dates back to divisions in the aftermath of the

Second World War, when the tartan-toting nostalgia of people of Scottish heritage abroad jarred on many inhabitants of a country facing imperial decline and political marginalisation. Yet as the appeal of historic pageantry has shrunk in Scotland, it has continued to grow elsewhere, even in countries with no Scottish diaspora to speak of. Continental Europe is home to a wide range of celebratory Scottish activity, from the Scottish Festival at Salzburg to the Alba Festival in Grasse, Scots Fair in Ghent and Scotfest in Tilburg. 'Highland Cathedral' – for some a candidate for a future Scottish national anthem – was composed by two Germans for a German Highland Games, while Highland Games in France can sometimes involve bizarre fusion events, such as the tossing of a giant champagne cork.

Scottish shops, restaurants and tourist mementos can be found throughout Europe, where they are often confused with Irish culture, nationality or brands. Some sixty Scottish dance societies cater to the enthusiasm for Scottish dancing, among them the Munich Caledonians and the Schiehallion Dance School of St Petersburg, while historical re-enactment groups such as Montgomerie's Highlanders from the Czech Republic underline the enduring appeal of Romantic military Scotland.

For a country that has not been a nation state in its own right for more than three centuries, Scotland retains extraordinarily close ties with other nations. Whether or not it makes enough of these relationships is a moot point. The Scotland consumed overseas is the stirring landscape of mountain and flood, animated with glimpses of the primitive, virile and supernatural. Global Scotland is Romantic Scotland. Diana Gabaldon's *Outlander* novels would perhaps not have sold 50 million copies and spawned seven television series if they had been set in Edinburgh's New Town and starred Adam Smith and David Hume. The *Harry Potter* films, too, place Hogwarts in the heart of a bleak Highland Scotland, a baronial fantasy reached by Jacobite steam train over the Glenfinnan viaduct. And in the ostensibly historical *Mary Queen of Scots* (2018), the moment Mary steps outside her palace she finds herself in a landscape of rugged and vertiginous slopes, far from cultivation or industry.

This mythical, Romantic version of Scotland is a world away from the modern Scotland of reality, a nation of space industries, *Grand Theft Auto* and Dolly the Sheep (on display in the National Museum of Scotland since her death in 2003). Bringing myth and reality closer together, while acknowledging the pageantry and power of Scotland's landscape, culture and history, will be a key task for a new international Scotland – whether it remains within the United Kingdom or departs.

Image Credits

p.7 Callanish stones / Credit: Chmee2/Wikimedia; p.8 Cairn at Maes Howe / Credit: Chronicle/Alamy Stock Photo; p.14 Bronze helmet / Credit: Airminded/ Wikimedia; p.19 Traprain Law treasure / Public domain; p.22 Dumbarton Rock and Castle / Credit: Yale Center for British Art, Paul Mellon Collection; p.36 Battle of Brunanburh / Credit: Chronicle/Alamy Stock Photo; p.41 St Margaret's chapel ; p.51 Melrose Abbey / Public domain; p.53 Monymusk Reliquary / Public domain; p.54 Seannachie recites the royal genealogy / Credit: Corpus Christie College, Cambridge; p.59 Alexander III's seal / Public domain; p.67 King John (Forman Armorial) / Credit: Alamy; p.72 Coronation Chair / Public domain; p.83 Declaration of Arbroath / Credit: National Records of Scotland; p.94 Hammermen of Glasgow crest/ Credit: Hammermen of Glasgow / p.96 Stirling Castle 360 Panorama / Credit: Philip Game/Alamy Stock Photo; p.98 Holyrood Palace / Public domain; p.102 John Leslie map of Scotland, 1578 / Credit: Yale Center for British Art, Paul Mellon Collection; p.103 Wolf's Lair / Wikimedia Commons; p.107 The invasion of Edinburgh, 1544 / Public domain; p.108 John Knox, portrait of 1572 / Public domain; p.110 Francis and Mary coin / Public domain; p.111 Mary, Queen of Scots / Credit: Royal Collection Trust; p.115 Edinburgh Castle by John Slezer 1693 / Credit: National Library of Scotland; p.120 The downsitting (i.e. beginning) of the Scottish Parliament, 1685 / Public domain; p.128 Exemplifation of the Act of Union / Public domain; p.130 James Francis Edward Stuart lands at Peterhead, 1715 / Public domain; p.132 'Lost portrait' of Charles Edward Stuart / Credit: Scottish National Portrait Gallery; p.133 Culloden medal / Credit: Alamy; p.140 Adam Smith statue / Credit: Fotokon/Shutterstock; p.143 The Merchant Maiden Hospital / Credit: Wellcome Collection; p.147 The house at Rossville, Georgia / Public domain; p.151 Ice-making machine / Public domain; p.152 Scottish 'Highland' landscape / Credit: Artepics/Alamy Stock Photo; p.153 An episode from James Macpherson's Ossian / Credit: Philadelphia Museum of Art; p.157 Walter Scott's Bride of Lammermoor / Credit: Bristol Museum & Art Gallery; p.158 Balmoral in the 1850s / Credit: Aberdeen City Council (Archives, Gallery and Museums Collection); p.160 Jardine Matheson advert / Credit: Philg88/Wikimedia; p.163 Holmwood House / Credit: Shutterstock; p.165 Peter McLagan MP / Public domain; p.166 The Wallace Monument / Credit: Foto-jagla.de/Shutterstock; p.167 Scottish National Gallery. Credit: Shutterstock; p.168 Mackintosh style / Credit: Stapleton Collection/Bridgeman Images; p.171 Scottish National War Memorial / Credit: Wikimedia Commons; p.172 Logie Estate / Credit: Dundee City Archives; p.176 Scottish Pavilion / Public domain; p.177 Defused bomb / Credit: IWM; p.180 Hillman Imp / Credit: Smith Archive (Alamy); p.182 Beeching Cuts / Credit: Ben Brooksbank/Wikimedia; p.184 Christmas article / Credit: *West Lothian Adversiser* / p.188 Winnie Ewing / Credit: Tom King/ Mirrorpix; p.190 Poll tax protesters at Westminster / Credit: Associated Press (Alamy); p.195 Scottish Parliament / Credit: Ivan Vdovin/Alamy Stock Photo; p.203 Vivienne Westwood tartan / Credit: Trinity Mirror/Mirrorpix/Alamy Stock Photo; p.205 NY Tartan Week / Credit: New York Tartan Week.

Acknowledgements

My thanks and acknowledgements go to all those Scottish historians with whom I have conversed over the years, from the late Ross Mackenzie to Professor Dauvit Broun, who kindly looked over the early chapters of this book and made some very useful comments. My thanks go too to my colleagues in the University of Glasgow in the Office of the Vice-Principals and the Centre for Robert Burns Studies for their kindness and unflinching support. Lastly I would like to thank Ben Yarde-Buller and his team for the very careful and close attention they have paid to this book in the editing process and the hard work they have carried out on providing illustrations, maps and tables. I am always struck by how the world is full of distinguished people who admire Scotland more than it admires itself, and this book is dedicated to three of these friends in Prague, Professor Martin Próchazka MAE, Dr Mirka Horová and Dr Petra Johana Poncarová, who has spent two years at the University of Glasgow working with me on an MSCA Fellowship researching Ruaraidh Erskine of Mar and the growth of the Gaelic periodical press.

Life is short; history is long.

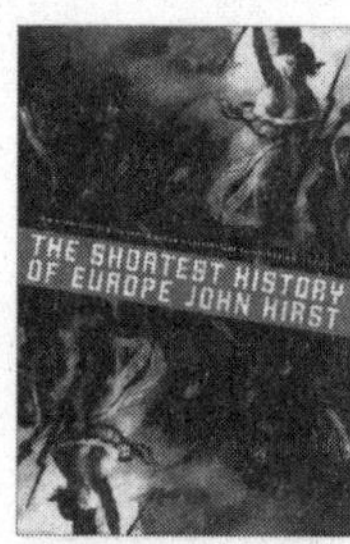

A FASCINATING JOURNEY THROUGH LIFE, THE UNIVERSE & EVERYTHING
The Shortest History of the
WORLD
DAVID BAKER
with a Foreword by John Green

STEPHEN BATES
THE SHORTEST HISTORY OF
THE CROWN

THE SHORTEST HISTORY OF ECONOMICS
ANDREW LEIGH

THE SHORTEST HISTORY OF
ITALY
ROSS KING

THE SHORTEST HISTORY OF
JAPAN
LESLEY DOWNER

THE SHORTEST HISTORY of
MUSIC
ANDREW FORD

THE SHORTEST HISTORY OF
ANCIENT ROME
Ross King

THE SHORTEST HISTORY OF FRANCE
Colin Jones

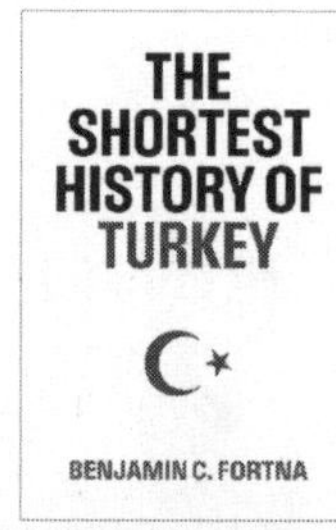

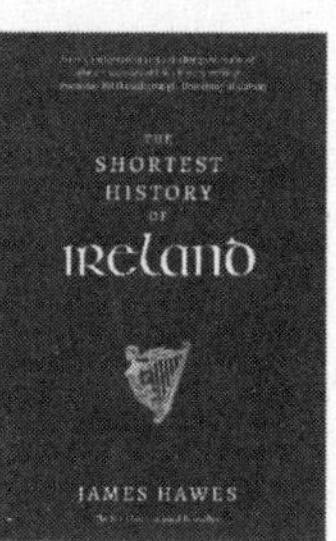

Explore the series
blackincbooks.com.au/series/shortest-history